Researching Race

Researching Race

Hasmita Ramji

Open University Press

Open University Press
McGraw-Hill Education
McGraw-Hill House
Shoppenhangers Road
Maidenhead
Berkshire
England
SL6 2QL

email: enquiries@openup.co.uk
world wide web: www.openup.co.uk

and Two Penn Plaza, New York, NY 10121–2289, USA

First published 2009

A catalogue record of this book is available from the British Library

ISBN 13: 9780335223015 (pb) 9780335223022 (hb)
ISBN 10: 033522301X (pb) 0335223028 (hb)

Library of Congress Cataloging-in-Publication Data
CIP data applied for

Typeset by YHT Ltd, London
Printed in the UK by Bell and Bain Ltd, Glasgow

The *McGraw-Hill* Companies

Contents

1 Introduction

Issues of race and racism and how they feature in contemporary society are topics of endless debate and fascination. The aftermath of the 'war on terror'[1] and continuous policy emphasis on creating inclusive multiculturalism in Western societies has seen the issue of race become increasingly important. This interest is reflected not only in academic and policy making institutions but also popular culture, as a cursory glance at any newspaper, television or radio programme schedule will demonstrate. Recent world events have not only created a new questioning around how race creates barriers among both global and national citizens but has bolstered a perception that it is pertinent to understanding a vast array of social issues. Accordingly there have been mounting calls to have a better understanding of what race is, how it affects people's lives and how society can circumvent 'racism'.[2] It has been social researchers that have been at the forefront of trying to answer these questions. This book is concerned with how researchers go about getting these answers. The book is particularly interested in the methodological problems likely to be encountered in certain aspects of race research and attempts to offer some strategies to deal with them.

Social research

It is useful to first place the research of race into the wider context in which it is discussed, the context of social research. Social scientists engage in research to understand the world around them. They employ a range of methods and are informed by a variety of theories. These in turn draw upon a certain understanding of the social world.[3] Within the social sciences there have been a number of disputes regarding what constitutes 'good' research.[4] It is possible to group these disputes around two overarching questions that need to be addressed in any research project: first, *what* is the object of research and, second, *how* can it be researched. In respect of race, these translate into, 'What is race' and 'How can it be measured and/or understood?' In the interests of simplicity, this volume shall refer to 'what' related questions as theoretical and 'how' related ones as methodological. However, it should be bore in mind that theoretical and methodological approaches are intimately connected, with each informing the other in any approach to social research. It is a central argument of this book that any research project involves an engagement with both theory and method.

While there are some basic principles of social research that have some universal relevance, each specialism has its own particular debates and pitfalls.[5]

Some universal aspects of doing research include:

- Formulating a researching question – this includes among others, clarifying the research field and operationalizing concepts.
- Collection of data – this includes among others accessing of databases, creating interview and/or survey questions and accessing respondents.
- Analysis – this includes among others the transcription and interpretation of data.
- Writing up and dissemination – this includes among others making the research findings accessible to non-experts in the field.
- Ethical considerations are also an important universal aspect of social research. As De Vaus (2002: 59) outlines, researchers have at least five ethnical responsibilities towards survey participants: voluntary participation, informed consent, no harm, confidentiality and privacy.

This introductory chapter will concentrate on the first of the points listed above which forms the most immediate task any researcher faces. Formulating a research question entails a reflection on how the concept of race is going to be operationalized in the research. This conceptualization in turn relates to the context in which the research of race is being done, both at a macro and micro level. In combination these help produce a research question.

Conceptualizing and operationalizing race

It is important to understand what is distinct about the concept of race so that the parameters of any research project can be set. It is also important to have a rationale for why any particular research project is concentrating on race and not ethnicity for instance. This involves a reflection on how race relates to other concepts and the society in which you live. The way race is conceptualized will have important implications for the methods selected.

Hutchinson (1996: 36) offers a classic distinction between race and ethnicity. 'Ethnicity is usually defined as membership in a subcultural group on the basis of country of origin, language, religion, or cultural traditions ... race on the other hand, is based on socially constructed definitions of physical appearances'. While the concepts are separate they often operate together (Goldberg 1993: 79; Bulmer and Solomos 2004). There has been an increased use of the term ethnicity over the term race in recent years, which for many is symptomatic of a broader change in the theoretical terrain in which these issues are discussed.[6] Bulmer and Solomos (2004: 7) comment 'what seems to characterise the contemporary period is, on the one hand, a complex spectrum of racisms, and, on the other, the fragmentation of the definition of previously perceived inclusive race identities, such as blackness as a political identity in favour of a resurgence of ethnic, cultural and religious differentiation'. Ethnicity is often thought to lend itself to carving finer social distinctions than race and to offer a more nuanced categorization of difference than race. Accordingly, it is thought to be more suited and useful to postmodern globalized societies. For this reason it is more closely aligned with individual notions of identity (Miles 1989; Hall 1991; Goldberg 1993; Miles and Torres 1996; Back and Solomos 1993).

This volume concentrates on race not ethnicity for a number of reasons which stem from an understanding of continued relevancy of race and an accompanying critique of alternative concepts like ethnicity for instance and the postmodern context in which they have developed that has emerged in recent years. For example, classifications by race have often been based on assumptions of superiority on the part of one group, grounded in social research and the study of these assumptions is part of the subject matter of the book. However, this volume is not advocating the perspective of critical race theory (that, although well known in the US, is markedly less known elsewhere), which is grounded in 'the uncompromising insistence that "race" should occupy the central position in any legal, educational, or social policy analysis' (Dardar and Torres 2004: 98). The belief in the pre-eminence of 'race' rather than other social differences such as social class, gender and sexuality is not advocated here, rather that the focus on race is a fruitful one. It is appreciated that race articulates itself in and through other social difference. Indeed it *may* make most sense when it is recognized as a gendered and classed phenomenon. However, as suggested elsewhere although it is useful to study interconnection of class, race and gender (as well as other stratifying factors such as age, locality and, in some contexts, religion) all these concepts have different antecedents and therefore can be usefully studied independently (Crompton 2006).

Ethnicity is certainly more prolific in recent writings. Aspects of it such as religion have received particular attention (Huntingdon 1996; Modood 2005; Dunn et al. 2007). However, while these aspects are important, they are not necessarily to be seen as wholly separate from discussions on race (Bonnett 1998; Hall 2000; Bhatt 2004). The perception of religion for example is also raced, the threat of Islamaphobia for instance is difficult to see without a racialized categorization of Muslims as non-white (Dunn et al. 2007). Moreover, it could be argued that the concept of ethnicity refers essentially to aspects traditionally associated with race (Hall 1992; Gilroy 1993). Sivanandan's (2006) concept of xenoracism argues that a feature of contemporary racism is the fear of strange races which fix ethnic features, such as symbolization of religious beliefs, like headscarfs, into somatic indicators of racial difference. Many writers have demonstrated that ethnicities are also liable to be appropriated as signifiers of permanently fixed boundaries (Mason 1994; Solomos and Back 1994; Smaje 1997; Bulmer and Solomos 1999; Aspinall 2001; Mullholland and Dyson 2001; Smith 2002). Bhatt (2004) suggests that, in a number of ways, current preoccupations with identity and hybridity in research on race and ethnicity may lead research in directions that close up important avenues of scholarship, rather than provide a basis for critical analysis to emerge and develop in fruitful directions. He places particular emphasis on the limitations of current theoretical preoccupations and fashions, and in doing so, he brings to the fore the need to analyse the historically specific contingent processes that shape what he calls 'race thinking' in contemporary societies.

Furthermore, other researchers have continued to argue that despite the postmodern allure of ethnicity, race continues to be a significant category of inquiry because of its continued social importance (Jenkins 1997; Bhattacharyya et al. 2002). Bashi (1998) makes a strong case that race matters because racial categories matter. The recognition that race does *not exist* has failed to lessen the impact of racialization as a mode for social organization and regulation of human society through economic and political privilege (Murji and Solomos 2005). Winant (2006: 986) argues that while a significant consensus exists that the concept of race lacks an objective basis, the concept persists as an idea, practice, identity and as part of the social structure. This means it will affect people's lives in real ways. Carter (2000) provides a good overview of the varying conceptualization of race in sociological research. Race is understood in this volume as a set of concepts and ideas, referring to social and political (but not biological) distinctions made between people. Race is an arbitrary social invention which forms part of the broader social context in which it has meaning and a force in practice. Its power lies in the force it has in people's thinking, actions and practices, and in their effect on the way things are organized (Knowles 2003). Referring to the arbitrary character of race Mason (1994) says that there are no races but there is racism. Mason continues that it is racism that establishes the social character of race. Accordingly, it is the nature of the forms of meaning, differentiation, exclusion and annihilation that establishes the social character of race.

Conceptualizing race

Race is a political and social construct. It is delineated by racism, a system that organizes the allocation of socio-economic power, exploitation and exclusion on the basis of a 'logic' that claims to ground the social and cultural differences which legitimize racialized exclusion in genetic and biological differences. This 'naturalizing effect' appears to make racial difference a fixed, scientific 'fact', unresponsive to change or reformist social engineering (Hall 1990): '"Ethnicity" by contrast, generates a discourse where difference is grounded in *cultural and religious features* ... [however] the articulation of difference with nature (biology and the genetic) is present, but displaced *through kinship and inter-marriage*' (Hall 2000: 222–3; emphasis in original).

The consensus then is that while race refers to a biological distinction, ethnicity refers to cultural, religious and kinship distinctions (Hall 2000; Mulholland and Dyson 2001). However, it would appear that such distinctions are not absolute and a researcher should be aware that such binaries of the biological and the cultural are not particularly helpful. Hall provides an insight here:

> Biological racism privileges markers like skin colour, but those signifiers have always also been used, by discursive extension, to connote social and cultural differences ... The biological referent is therefore never wholly absent from discourses of ethnicity, though it is more indirect. The more 'ethnicity' matters, the more its characteristics are represented as relatively fixed, inherent within a group, transmitted from generation to generation, not just by culture and education, but by biological inheritance, stabilized above all by kinship and endogamous marriage rules that ensure that the ethnic group remains genetically, and therefore culturally 'pure'.
>
> (Hall 2000: 223)

Hall's main point here is that the processes of biological and cultural differentiation through the categories of 'race' and ethnicity are interrelated not separate. The overlap and different theoretical approaches to categories (Smaje 1997) present some interesting dilemmas for the social researcher.

The danger of essentializing race through operationalization

This theoretical discussion, or the 'what' questions of race research, are intrinsically connected to the methodological discussion, or 'how' questions regarding race research. For those who see race as 'fixed' and thus an essential feature of any community, independent from social contexts (Solomos and Back 1994; Bulmer and Solomos 1996; Aspinall 2001) the best method for research has been most commonly associated with quantitative methodologies drawing on an empiricist tradition.[7] The essentialist position has become increasingly discredited in recent years by social constructionist approaches that argue that 'race' and ethnicity involve socially produced, heterogeneous and dynamic processes of being and becoming (see Brah 1996; Omi and Winant 1994); these approaches favour qualitative methodology. An important caveat is that quantitative approaches are not to be seen as exclusive to essentialist theorists of race, although there is a high level of association, this does not dictate an absolute or necessary association/ relationship. Also its fall from favour is not universal with, for instance, American sociologists still preferring surveying techniques associated with positivism (Payne 2007). This volume operates within the contention that race is created and meaningful in the context in which it features and researchers should be open to all methodology. Moreover any absolute distinction between methods (qualitative and quantitative) should be challenged. Crompton (2008) has constructively argued that the diametrically opposed positions revealed by the methodenstreit (disputes about methodology) are not in fact 'binaries' but interdependencies.

Gunaratnam (2003: 5) finds the often cited opposition between social constructionist approaches and materialist, realist or empiricist approaches that are said to be grounded in 'real' experience, as if experience somehow has a life of its own frustrating (see Brah et al. 1999; Hemmings 2002; Wuthnow 2002). Because of the social construction of race many researchers regard qualitative research as the only way of researching it. Only by finding out what people are thinking and how they are acting can we understand how race is made up in social processes. The experience of race in people's lives is dependent on how people perceive themselves, which is linked to socialization within particular cultures, the situations individuals find themselves in and the types of people they actually come into contact with. But there are many problems with qualitative approaches as Chapter 4 in this volume explores.

Alongside Stuart Hall (2000), Avtar Brah (1996) and Gail Lewis (2000), Gunaratnam (2003: 5) believes that social constructionists insights can be put to valuable use in understanding how experience is brought into being and has effects in specific social and interactional contexts. However, she also believes that failure to recognize the contingency and the ambivalent complexity of lived experience maintains an essentialist view of 'race', where experience can be seen to be wholly (pre)determined by racial categories, that are themselves construed as unchanging 'essences', cordoned off from social material and emotional (see Smaje 1997 for a critique of social constructionist approaches). Race may be thought of and thus experienced and acted upon as fixed.

On the other hand there is a school of thought within race researchers that argues that it is best to study race via quantitative methods precisely because they allow an impartial measurement of what race is. For example surveys allow us to understand people's attitudes to a number of statements or questions which are designed to measure and test people attitudes to race without necessarily asking them about it outright. Blending it into a social attitudes survey, for example, disguises the significance of the question and may well bring forth a more truthful answer. For some influential commentators the sample survey is the core methodological resource for sociology (Goldthorpe 2000; Halsey 2004).

However, in understanding race and measuring racism, a statistical approach, while essential, is fraught with difficulties. The counting of race, for example, has to go hand in hand with interpreting the meaning of race to different communities at different times and with considering the changing definitions of race. The changing conceptualization needs to be understood in the postmodern turn in the social sciences and the types of positions that this has legitimated in social research. While constructionist accounts are valorized positivist accounts are not (see Savage and Burrows (2007) for a critique of surveys). However, it is worth noting that many official bodies including government agencies still prefer statistically based evidence.

Pause for reflection: Getting somewhere in the qualitative and quantitative debate

As Payne et al. (2004) argue that there has been a concern in recent years about the lack of quantitative methods being employed in social research, including research on race, by influential institutions and organizations like the Economic and Social Research Council (ESRC). This eventually resulted in a change to the ERSC training for PhD students. They argue that while methodological pluralism is increasingly appreciated as a good thing in contemporary social research and while many researchers seem to embrace pluralism at a theoretical level, they do not practice it. The lack of quantitative method expertise and popularity in the UK in particular is marked compared to the US.

For them it is important to push the pluralist agenda forward because the dichotomy between 'quantitative' and 'qualitative' methods, is a useful shorthand but does not stand up to scrutiny and thus does not really provide a foundation for debate (Bryman 2008).

This problematization fits into the argument throughout the book that the complicated nature of social existence should merit some diverse research.

In a very interesting response to Payne et al.'s article May (2005) points to a parallel debate in the *British Journal of Sociology* regarding the methodological positions adopted by current sociologists. The exchange provides a way of expanding on the point made in this volume and by others that the debate about utilizing a wide range of methods is related to the belief that social research should have relevance for the outside world. As Johnson (2004) and Lauder et al. (2004) among others note, anxieties about the relevance of research are prominent at the moment. The debate also reveals anxieties about the complexities of relations between the academy and the state (e.g., ESRC). Surveying the journals there does seem to be dearth quantitative methods, May notes, but not in America and elsewhere. However, he deduces that this is symptomatic of a lack of intellectual positions, not a lack of technical skills. This debate has been carried on other key international scholarly journals, for example *Sociology* (2007 Special Edition), and by key sociologists, for example Crompton in *Sociology* (2008).

- It is useful to spend some time at this juncture to reflect on how the dilemmas around essentialist/non-essentialist, and qualitative and quantitative methodological debates are linked to wider controversies in current sociology. It what ways do you think the current debates in race research are linked to these wider debates?

There is a tension for the race researcher between the theoretical perception of race as non-essentialist and socially constructed and employing research methods which however unintentionally fix the meaning of race so that it can be studied (Rattansi 1994; Murji and Solomos 2005). As Nayak (2006: 403) has recently reflected, 'to engage with researching race is to run the risk of reifying the very thing we are seeking to deny'. Even social constructionist accounts, Nayak asserts, inescapably 'take "race" as an ontological baseline – historically and politically situated perhaps, but ultimately identifiable and knowable' (also see Ali 2004a: 324). There is a continual theoretical and methodology struggle for the race researcher to articulate a new voice for speaking race that at the same time renders it mute. Butler (1994) in her work on gender has identified the strain between social constructionism and its reliance upon the ontological security of a knowable object, resulting in a mundane sort of violence. This is apparent in both positivist and hermeneutic (interpretive) understanding.

Gunaratnam (2003: 18) similarly argues that at the epistemological level there can be related tensions between the need to work with highly defined categories of race in order to undertake research that challenges social inequalities, and the recognition that such categories are socially and historically contingent and situated (for a debate about race categories in research, see Modood et al. 2002 and Smith 2002). These issues are further interwined with lived experiences of 'race' and ethnicity and identity politics (Clifford 2000). The drive towards categorization is indicative of tensions involved in researching race in the current climate. The reliance and use of racial categories in research can in itself involve the research in reproducing dominant conceptions of 'race' and ethnicity (Stanfield and Dennis 1993; Smith 2002). Dominant conceptions refer to the 'particular political formations of social meaning (discourses) that produce "race" and ethnicity as discrete, homogeneous, fixed categories of difference' (Gunaratnam 2003: 28). Gunaratnam (2003) argues that researchers are in a 'treacherous bind' (Radhakrishan 1996) in researching questions of race, because we are thinking with concepts at the limit (Derrida 1981). In this respect, Lather (2001) points to the need for a 'doubled' research practice, in which researchers need to work both with and against racial and ethnic categories at the levels of epistemology and methodology. Gunaratnam (2003) usefully outlines how a researcher can work with the inadequate racial categories that are to hand, while also finding ways to identifying and disrupting the ways in which these same categories can 'essentialize' race. These issues are explored in greater detail in Chapter 2.

Pause for reflection

How do you go about researching something like 'race' which you are simultaneously trying to demonstrate has no absolute basis?

Some ways forward

So how can we conceptualize and operationalize race while continuing to challenge its existence? Nayak (2006) proposes 'post-race' analysis, which positions 'race' as a series of performances and repeated effects which deny any ontological stability or security as a possible solution to this dilemma for race researchers. Post-race writing adopts an anti-foundational perspective which claims that 'race is a fiction only ever given substance to through the illusion of performance, action and utterance, where repetition makes it appear as-if-real' (Nayak 2006: 416).

Nayak (2006: 419) further elaborates that whiteness or blackness as race are not attached to respective white and black bodies but rather that race signs are encoded into everyday practice. The post-race perspective also enables a researcher to see that signifiers of black and white are relational and mutually constitutive. Fanon's work on the dynamics of colonialism in French occupied Algiers provides a good illustration of how a post-race perspective can be used by a social researcher. For Fanon there is no recourse to blackness or whiteness as 'proper objects', but rather it is an ontological critique of arbitrary sign-making system that makes them appear true: 'For not only must the black man be black: he must be black in relation to the white man' ([1952] 1970: 77). By helping us 'undo' race by breaking links between race and bodies the post-race perspective can help a researcher maintain a non-essentialist position on race by ensuring that it has no natural basis. Researchers keen to rewrite race in the light of post-race thinking face an awkward challenge: how do we put post-race theory into post-race practice? Nayak (2006: 424) argues that the complicated task for contemporary ethnographers is not to ignore race and racism by constructing black, deracialized accounts, but to rewrite race outside of its attendant categories by using an imaginative post-race vocabulary.

> To essentialise is to impute a fundamental, basic, absolutely necessary constitutive quality to a person, social category, ethnic group, religious community, or nation. It is to posit falsely a timeless continuity, a discreteness or boundedness in space, and an organic unity. It is to imply an internal sameness and external difference or otherness
>
> (Werbner 1997: 228)

It is worth pointing out at this juncture that the post-race perspective at present remains a relatively unclear, diffuse cluster of ideas. As it's entry in Ratcliffe's (2004) *'Race', Ethnicity and Difference* suggests, there is as yet 'no real agreement as to how best define this term'. It is also controversial because for some researchers it risks the emergence of an apolitical 'racelessness' which fails to recognize older political gains and structural inequalities (Bulmer and Solomos 2004): 'If we dissolve the category of race, for instance, it becomes difficult to claim the experience of racism' (Alexander and Mohanty 1997: xvii).

Another useful way that researchers formulated for conceptulizing race is by placing it in the context in which it is to be studied, in particular to understand that the way racism operates in a given context defines race. Knowles (2003) in a her book *Race and*

Social Analysis advocates such a position, arguing that a researcher can best find strategies for conceptualizing race by seeing it as created in the tapestry of life. It is impossible to understand the meaning of race without a social context. As Knowles (2005) argues 'trying to pick race ... out of a set of circumstances is like tracing a thread through an intricate tapestry: the thread has no special meaning on its own, but it forms a vital constituent of the overall picture which would not make sense without it' (p. 109). Using Knowles's paradigm any race researcher should see race as operating on a structural, social and individual level, and should formulate research question and conceptualizations accordingly. This perspective would enable an understanding that race is only meaningful in a given context and is defined by processes of prejudice and exclusion.

This involves understanding that race is not an absolute category, but recognizing that in a research project one is trying to understand how 'race' happens in a particular case. Thus here research projects do need to create a static concept to operate with and establish whether their findings have any resonance. A case study approach here is useful, where the research attempts to understand a social phenonomen in a given context.

Case study approach

Robson (2007: 27) provides a succinct summary of the advantages and disadvantages of this *case study approach*.

Advantages

1   Studying a single case (or a small number of cases) gives the opportunity to carry out a study in depth, which can capture complexities, relationships and processes.
2   It strongly encourages the use of multiple methods of collecting data, and of multiple data sources.
3   The boundaries of the study (e.g., the amount of time involved and context covered) are flexible, and can often be tailored to the time and resources you have available.
4   It is less artificial and detached than traditional approaches such as experiments and surveys.
5   It can be used for a wide variety of research purposes and for widely different types of cases.

Disadvantages

1   The credibility of generalizations from case studies is often challenged. It depends on a different logic from that familiar in surveys.
2   Case studies typically seek to focus on situations as they occur naturally and hence observer effect caused by the presence of the researcher can be problematic.
3   The flexible nature of case study design means that you have to be prepared to modify your approach, depending on the results of your involvement. It can become difficult to keep to deadlines.

In their recent study of race and ethnicity in the British Police Force for example, Holdaway and O'Neil (2006) demonstrate the usefulness of conceptualizing race in specific contexts. They argue that being 'black' in the police force has a specific fragility and exclusivity which only makes sense in the context of employment in the police force, which has a specific historical and organizational circumstance, particularly relating to race. The Macpherson Inquiry infamously described it as institutionally racist. They concur with Brubaker et al. (2004) that it is difficult to sustain a neat analytical distinction between 'race' and 'ethnicity' when considering 'police ethnicity'. The Black Police Association presents their membership as united by a single experience of racism. But in fact Asian and black police officers make up the majority of the non-white workforce and have many divisions within their ranks as they have with white officers, but they project a unified racial identity 'black' because they recognize the significance of this in the police force.

An effective strategy to conceptualize race is to formulate a research question which enables the researcher to set limitations on what aspect of race they are going to research, understanding it in that particular context and how it influences that particular social moment. Definitive knowledge about race is not possible but one can strive to know as much as possible in the particular remit one has set oneself. Race is defined by the particular circumstances it is set in.

The wider context of conceptualizing race

The way race features in society will be reflective in any research project. As a researcher it is important to reflect on how our social context may influence what we consider to be important to research.

Interest in researching race has existed throughout the history of social science, and the type and methods of acquiring this knowledge has reflected the characteristics of society. This is evidenced in the work of explorers, missionaries and anthropologists and so have various methodological approaches to researching it.

In particular the conceptualization, 'findings' or purpose of the research is only understood with reference to the social context. These methodological approaches have been guided by theories and the theories must be understood from a sociological perspective. From the eugenics movement to early anthropology, knowledge about race arguably said more about the societies the researchers came from than the people and the societies they were studying. What was considered as acceptable understanding about the nature of race in the past was often quite different to current notions, just as many contemporary ideas of race would have been dismissed as nonsense in earlier times. Indeed in studying race over time the most obvious research 'finding' is the relative nature of race. What is seen as and defined as legitimate understanding of the nature of race varies according to the particular social context in which it occurs.

Pause for reflection: The cultural and historical relativity of race research

It is easy to think of examples of race knowledge/research findings on race which although not seen as legitimate now were quite acceptable in the past.

Scientific approaches to the notion of racial differences and hierarchies are seen as originating in the Enlightenment period and offer a good illustration of this point. Enlightenment thinking aligned civilization with white European culture, and judged other cultural and racial groups as inferior in terms of rationality and morality. Bowling and Phillips (2002) refer to Gobineau's 1853 essay on *The Inequality of Human Races* in which 'negroes' are described as having mental faculties that are 'dull or even non-existent' and as killing 'willingly, for the sake of killing'. Later in the nineteenth century, Lombroso argued in a similar vein that there was a clear link between race and crimes: 'many of the characteristics found in savages, and in the coloured races; are also to be found in habitual delinquents'.

Race of course has attracted a great deal of interest over the centuries. However, the nature of this interest has reflected the preoccupations of a particular society. This results in a differing focus at different times. For example, as we will discuss in Chapter 2, the period of colonialism was marked by a period of race research in Western societies which was primarily focused on 'proving' the existence of a race hierarchy which situated whites at the pinnacle, non-whites at the bottom and thus justified the exploitative colonial relations (Fanon 1986; Gilroy 1993).

The fact that knowledge about race and acceptable race research practice varies, from place to place and time to time highlights the importance of social reaction in determining what knowledge is. There is no particular knowledge that is truth in itself – knowledge becomes acceptable only if society defines it as such.

Contextualizing current fascination: The whys and whats of race research

It is useful to connect this discussion to more recent research on race. This in turn allows an avenue into understanding how the purpose of race research differs.

The current fascination with race reflects our current interest in identity, multiculturalism and difference. These are, of course, mutually related phenomena. Identity is usefully understood as a subjective perception of self, influenced by cultural markers such as religion, language as well as ethnicity and race. Increasingly Western societies are asking themselves questions about what their identity is, for example what constitutes an American identity. Our curiosity to know about how people who are different from us experience social life may explain its high profile. It may serve to confirm our own sense of identity, or indeed our own prejudices. In other words, we are fascinated to know about other races, because our sense of identity is heavily inscribed by it and knowing how we differ from others confirms our sense of self.

Knowles' framework discussed above is useful here. At an individual level Knowles (2003) argues that our identity is increasingly understood through subjective understanding/perception of racial and ethnic positioning. Identity is about belonging, about what you have in common with some people and what differentiates you from others. At its most basic it gives you a sense of personal location, the stable core to your individuality. At a social level, race is also about your social relationships, your complex involvement with others, and in the modern world it is thought that these have become ever more complex and confusing. Race and ethnicity provide an important window into how people understand themselves and each other.

Similarly, at a structural level we are concerned with who belongs to our American identity for example; the attempt to make identities 'multicultural' seems to be a priority if we are to live with difference and harness difference among social groups and different races as productive elements and not a potential source of alienation, which can create and nurture suicide bombers and terrorism in our midst. While most groups live together in remarkably similar existences, it is those incidents that mark out racial difference and conflict which tend to occupy media coverage and hold popular attention the most. For example the attention given to ethnic gang violence, Yardie drug traffickers, religious fundamentalists and veiled women. It also is related to the current war on terror and the threat that racialized others are perceived to pose to Western ways of life. Race research is usually preceded by the perception of race as a problem.

The type of research done and the knowledge it produces is incredibly important in Western societies where people have little interaction with people outside their own racial groups, particular in their private lives (Essed 1991; Frankenberg 1993; Ramji 2007). Thus the knowledge produced by race researchers in institutions like universities may be the only information they have. It is a mistake to assume that multicultural societies operate with a wealth or accurate knowledge about the racial groups that make them up.

Bulmer and Solomos (2004: 6) argue that part of the context for the transformation of research agendas that we have seen in recent years has been the growing evidence of diversity in the experiences of ethnic minority and immigrant groups. The differentiation in economic position, gender, migration history, political participation and perceptions of social citizenship are significant among minority ethnic groups, and they are becoming increasingly evident.

Differentiation of socio-economic and political position has coincided with a rise in what has been called 'identity politics'. Such developments have been reflected in the emergence of new areas of scholarly debate and research in relation to the study of race and racism, particularly focusing on the cultural politics of difference or the politics of recognition, carrying with it calls for a new pluralism, radical democracy and empowerment.

Pause for reflection: Race as a social problem

An important dimension to any race research is the politically charged nature of the field in which it operates.

In most countries race is an important factor in determining citizenship; this is linked to ideas discussed earlier about identity and multiculturalism. From discussions about the right of third and fourth generation immigrants to call themselves British or Australian, to the rights of refugees to settle, to the expansion of the EU leading to East Europeans taking 'our' jobs, race debates in Western societies are politically charged. In the midst of public mobilization and political anxiety the 1970s, for example, saw the introduction of a series of legislation designed to restrict immigration to Great Britain. It is widely accepted that the target was primarily non-white immigrants.

The contact with different races was not only thought to threaten 'identities' but to hasten social conflict, different races were perceived as incompatible. There was widespread hostility to the influx of 'coloured' immigrants to particular areas of Britain, the best known example being Enoch Powell's 1968 speech predicting 'rivers of blood' on the streets of Britain as a result of immigrants from Asia and the West Indies. Although Powell's comments were widely condemned, when Margaret Thatcher became prime minister in 1979 her sympathetic comments over white fears of being 'swamped' by 'alien cultures' reflected similar sentiments. In the early 1980s the inner city disorders in many parts of Britain, most notable Brixton, Bristol, Liverpool and Manchester, lent support to the stereotype of black youths as disorderly and criminal.

- List other such speeches made by high profile public figures.
- Why do you think such speeches continue to be made?

It is helpful to work through contemporary controversies to bring to the fore why you want to study the subject.

- What types of events create scare stories around race?
- How is the issue of race connected to other concerns in contemporary society?
- What positive stories are there? Are there any common elements to them? How were these findings acquired?

Race has been part of the de-essentialist critique theorized as involving political processes of classification (Miles 1982, 1989; Omi and Winant 1994). Race has been seen as variegated social category that is in a constant state of production and negotiation with other forms of difference, and within specific social historical and interactional arenas, while also serving to constitute these arenas.

At the same time, however uncomfortable, methods that employ essentialist categories of 'race' do have some level of resonance with lived experience and this is something that we need to both address and interrogate. As argued elsewhere, the degree of resonance between the categories and lived experiences and identifications can be influenced by political and funding agendas (Aspinall 2001).

Race research reflects perceptions of social reality and purpose of research

This difficulty of conceptualization and particularly its relationship to other contemporary popular concepts also comes to the fore in how one can understand the formulation of a research question and methods for answering it. This, of course, is linked to why the research should be done.

Bulmer and Solomos (2004: 3) write

From the earliest stages of scholarly research in sociology about race, there has been some tension about what the focus should be. Should the core concern be to study the relations between racial and ethnic groups in specific social environments? Or should the focus be on the impact of processes of discrimination and exclusion, and their impact on minority communities?

Researchers have been pulled in many directions. John Rex, a leading British researcher in race and ethnic relations for the past five decades, in 1979 wrote that

a race researcher was pulled in the following:

1   There was the demand that research should be put in the service of policy, as though there was a consensus about ends, and the only questions which need to be rsearched were about means;
2   there was the pull for a retreat into academic theorizing, in which the research questions asked are not seen as necessarily related to the issues that made race relations a public issue.
3   there was the option of rejecting academic research in this field as a whole, in favour of political activism or action oriented work.
(Rex 1979, quoted in Bulmer and Solomos 2004: 5)

His typology of different approaches captured some of the recurrent problems that social researchers working in this field have had to come to terms with. In recent years Bulmer and Solomos note a move to a fixation with theoretical abstraction and textual and cultural analysis. It is not the position of this book that a researcher cannot do all, or should not aspire to do all, rather that these are the typical forms research on race have fallen into. The strategies for answering each of these should also be open to methods.

It is an assumption of this book that research on race is important to do, it is not concerned with making an argument for it, because contemporary events seem to make this self-apparent and others have done this more effectively (for example Gunaratnam 2003). While one could speculate on why there is such a fascination, and many have done so, the methods by which one can acquire greater knowledge of these areas, that is how one can go about researching race in society is given less attention.

These concerns are certainly not new but are in evidence through the history of race research, for example in the work of W. E. B. DuBois, Robert Park in the US, we can trace the history back to the twentieth century (Bulmer and Solomos 2004: 2). 'Throughout this history, however, there has been intense debate about what the focus of such research should be and on the appropriateness of conceptual and methodological tools for analyzing the changing and evolving patterns of race and ethnic relations in contemporary societies' (2004: 5).

Many theorists see race as a process, a set of discursive practices which continually produce and regulate 'race' as a concept and social category (see for example Solomos and Back 1996; Knowles 2003; Solomos 2003). It is difficult to make this tangible and concrete, as we are now aware that this concept is continually debated in theory, discourse, policy and the everyday. But we know it is important and has real concrete meaning and effect through claims to raced belonging and racism.

It has proven notoriously difficult to pin down the fundamental questions that researchers should be asking. Part of the reason for this lies in the diverse range of theoretical perspectives and methodologies that have emerged over the past two decades or so (Bulmer and Solomos 2004: 3). While there has been a proliferation of theoretical and empirically focused accounts there has been little dialogue about the methodologies to be used in developing research in this field.

Politicized nature of race research

Another specific difficulty with doing research on race is the highly policitized nature of the field as touched upon earlier. What is meant here is the heavy influence political agendas have had in the shaping and challenging of race research. For example race is now accepted as an important source of social inequality and this is a powerful pull for social scientists seeking to understand social injustice. Most research is concerned not only with understanding the social world but with changing it for the better. As Marx famously wrote, the point of theory is not to understand the social world but to change it. However, the crucial importance given to race also means that the areas of research, that is what is to be researched and how, have been influenced by political debates and landscapes. For example there are a limited number of funding bodies nearly all of whom are government funded and who in turn make funding available for certain projects.

Pause for reflection

Using the Internet make a list of the organizations that fund social science research and where they get their resources. Write down the most recent or most high profile projects they have funded and compare and contrast your findings with your fellow students.

- What commonalities are apparent in the 'priorities' of these funding bodies?
- What are the commonalities and difference in the projects they have funded?
- Can you relate this to significant events that have happened in recent years?
- Consider the question of whether events determine politicians' race agendas and or whether politicians determine race agenda – what are the implications for a race researcher?

Indeed a great deal of social research is driven by social need, for example government funding for issues such as racial discrimination in the education or employment sector. The following are good examples of case studies of social research which have received a great deal of media attention: black boys' schooling, Asian Muslim employment status and Criminal Justice treatment of black and, increasingly, Asian youth.

It seems important to understand why this is the case not only to help those people located in these groups but also to help the wider society understand why this is occurring and the devastating effects it can have on society as a whole. This is also related to why so much controversy surrounds the field, as different governments have influenced race research in varying ways. This theme is considered in more detail later in this book.

Pause for reflection

Historical and contemporary government-led initiatives have had a huge influence on what research has been done and how

Bulmer and Solomos (2004: 3) note that race has been an area of research that has been closely linked to wider policy and political debates in societies such as the US and UK among others. Du Bois's makes an early observation of this in his work, *The Philadelphia Negro*. Such linkages to everyday political and policy considerations have been an important feature of race research over the past century.

Dilemmas for the social researcher

This of course brings to the fore a number of important and distinct dilemmas for the social researcher:

- Who will fund the research? What sort of obligations will this entail? For example, gaining accessing to a data-set may mean that one has to be affliated to certain organizations for example, trade unions.
- What are the factors motivating your research question? Contemporary popularity? Does this mean that more legitimate/pressing areas of race research are being neglected? Think about areas that are covered in other areas but are not done is race. Does this perpetuate a focus on problems when conducting research on race?

Bulmer and Solomos (2004: 4) argue 'the experience of research during the period since the 1960s has brought to the fore questions about the funding of research on race and racism: who does the funding; who carries out the research; what the key findings are; and how they are used in public policy debates and in the mass media. A particular area of concern from the 1960s onwards, in both the US and the UK to take just two examples, related to the depiction of black people in terms of 'social problems' of deviancy and marginality. This was seen as partly the result of government policy agendas and the availability of research funding. Money was available to study racial and ethnic minorities as social problems or culturally deprived communities, but not as cultures with their own normatic values, behavioural patterns and institutions.

This book's focus

This book is concerned with providing a strategic guide to doing research on race. It will engage with both theoretical and methodological issues in an accessible format, using timely illustrations and case studies to facilitate understanding in some key areas of current concern. The volume's main aim is to provide readers with some practical advice on doing such research, and theoretical, epistemological and methodological considerations are focused on as and when appropriate. It is also important to point out that the book is not seeking to be a comprehensive guide, any book attempting to do so would be thwarted given the sheer volume of material and high level of debate in the area.

Rather it limits its focus to a few issues which can then used by researchers as a springboard to consider a myriad other issues.

What follows is an attempt to tackle some of the issues that a researcher of race may come across. While I will attempt to review a number of points and give a balanced view it is rather inevitable that I will be unable to review all the debates. Accordingly, bearing in mind the relativity of race and race research, Chapter 2 considers the history of race research and examines its implications for contemporary research. If Chapters 1 and 2 are about deciding the focus of your research and the question(s) to which you are seeking answers, Chapters 3 and 4 are concerned with ways to seek answers, and Chapter 5 is about analysing and interpreting these answers so you can tell others what you have found.

This book operates on the understanding that researchers should question 'race' as a category and thus highly prescriptive 'solutions' to the challenges of researching 'race' become untenable. Thus, rather than solutions, it is concerned with offering guidelines for strategies which enable the researcher to move forward.

Summary

It is important to recognize that race researchers will be operating with a contested category. Moreover one of the first dilemmas they will encounter is the fact that race is not a stable or homogenous category but is best seen as being produced in social contexts. In turn these social contexts should be seen as produced and animated by changing, complicated and uneven interactions between social processes and individual experience. It is important to establish this element of commonality and difference with other types of social research from the outset, because its specificity must not guide one to believe that race research is a distinct field that has no relation to other epistemological, theoretical and methodological dilemmas encountered in other fields. This would artificially essentialize race and hamper attempts at researching race. Indeed as the chapters make clear race, research is simultaneously related to other social research areas and their methodological quagmire, and it also has some unique properties due to the way it exists in the society in which it is studied.

It is important to note that these dilemmas must be seen as ongoing and to be engaged with throughout the research process. There are not necessarily any solutions for the difficulties likely to be encountered in race research, and most certainly no solutions without negative consequences elsewhere, but there are strategies which have proven to be useful for established researchers which can be drawn upon. The particular dilemmas any researcher faces will be influenced by the choice of topic, theoretical preferences, practical considerations and research methods selected.

Summary of suggestions

1   Consider what is motivating you to research the aspect of race you are focusing on. Social research should have a relevance to the wider society, and it is a great advantage of race research that it provides this. What do you want to explore or explain?

2   Formulate an understanding of race in your research that takes on board the fact that it is not fixed, but varies in meaning and manifestation between social contexts.

3   Link the commonalities as well as the specifics of race research to other types of social research to aid your argument.

4   Theory and method are not separable, so how one approaches race will influence the methods selected and in turn the methods one selects will influence theory. It is important for researchers to be as open to everything as possible.

Further reading

Alexander, C. (2006) Introduction: mapping the issues, *Ethnic and Racial Studies*, 29(3): 397–410 provides a good sophisticated discussion on what she terms 'the why, how and when' of doing race research, but with specific regard to ethnography.

Bulmer, M. and Solomos, J. (1996) Introduction: race, ethnicity and the curriculum, *Ethnic and Racial Studies*, 19(4): 777–88.

De Vaus, D. (2002) *Surveys in Social Research*. London: Routledge. This provides excellent generic advice for designing a research proposal.

McNeil, P. and Chapman, S. (2005) *Research Methods*, 3rd edn. London: Routledge. This book is a good succinct introduction to the evolution of methodology within sociology, from its founding years to contemporary practice.

Twine, F. W. and Warren, J. W. (eds) (2000) *Racing Research, Researching Race: Methodological Dilemmas in Critical Race Studies*. New York: New York University Press. This book provides a good overview of the nature of this debate from an American perspective.

Notes

1   It is important to see this as a response to the incidents of 11 September 2001 in America and 7 July 2006 in Britain.

2   There has been a difference among countries, however, regarding the perception of how race matters, and this has impacted on what sorts of issues are argued to need more research attention. This book focuses on Western societies.

3   See McNeil and Chapman (2005) for a good overview.

4   See recent debates in the *Sociology* journal and *British Journal of Sociology* 2007/08.

5   Troyna has described the act of researching race as 'a tricky business' (1995: 386) and provides a good articulation of this point in his neat summary of the numerous points of contention that have inspired a series of methodological debates in the area of race research (Nayak 2006: 412).

6   For example the postmodern climate described by Westwood and Rattansi (1996) and subsequent arrival of post-race theory (Nayak 2006).

7   These are well rehearsed (see for example Gunaratnam 2003; and Solomos and Bulmer 2004) but it is still necessary to go over, albeit briefly, in a book of this nature.

2 Theoretical and methodological debates in the research of race

Method and theory are intimately connected in race research, as in any social research. This chapter is interested in exploring how the emergence, development and application of different social theory has impacted on the way race has been researched. The aim of this chapter is to enable contemporary researchers to understand the epistemological limitations certain theories may pose to the different stages of a research project; how they are linked to certain methods which in themselves may be limiting for a researcher; and how they can use these reflections to formulate strategies for negotiating these limitations.

For a social researcher it is important to know and understand the origin and development of social theory which ultimately guides any research project methodology. This is because it may have implications, however unintentional, for the type of research done on race.

This chapter will focus on the following to elaborate this discussion:

1　The development of social theory and 'race' research in the modern period which is characterized by colonial expansion and the exclusion of non-Western, non-white racial experiences in generating (a bias set of) knowledge.
2　The implications of this for a race researcher, and strategies that have been developed by researchers to move forward.
　　It is useful to explore these strategies along two broad themes:
　　- To develop a non-Western based set of theories to guide research on race through developing an alternative archive of knowledge. This chapter will focus on the approach advocated by Smith (1999), which aims to allow 'raced' communities to articulate themselves on their own terms, what she terms 'indigenous research'. For many researchers this also entails a move away from the scientific rationale and empiricism in conventional race research to qualitative research.
　　- A related pathway within this strategy is to counterbalance biases in traditional theory and methodology relating to race research by studying whiteness, a race that has traditionally been neglected due to its perceived invisibility.
　　- A second strategy has found that the best way forward is working subversively with existing dominant concepts.

The key difficulty of researching race for many writers is that the frameworks developed to do so (from the conceptualization to the analysis) are not neutral, but are located in Western societies and consequently draw on a particular historical and cultural heritage, a heritage which excludes non-white others, is culturally Euro-centric and throws up particular problems for a researcher interested in researching race either within Western societies (which is the concern of this volume) or without (which has been the concern of others, for example Gandi 1998). The changes associated with the processes of globalization, postmodernity and postcolonialism[1] have stimulated a critique of Western frameworks of knowledge about race. These changes are important for understanding the changing presence and conceptualization of racial groups in society and the methodologies appropriate for researching them.

Modernity and race research

Social science, including the theory and methodological approaches that are specific to it, developed rapidly during the period termed 'modernity'.[2] Modernity has been criticized in a number of ways for the type of research it conducted on race and the subsequent knowledge it produced. Modernity was accompanied by a philosophy of a period called the Enlightenment. This placed a heavy emphasis on science to discover social truths. Around this era research was conducted and guided by the belief that there were truths around race to be discovered. A major impact for methodological approaches was the preference for empirical methods as these were perceived as more scientifically valid.

However, the truth sought about 'race' reflected the social, political and economic situation of modern society, specifically colonial expansion. Agnew (1999) has called this the 'geo-political imagination', through which 'race' in a context of colonialism was used to map and give politicized meaning to distinctions between different parts of the world, and was used to classify and distinguish differences within colonial populations (Rattansi and Westwood 1994; Bauman 1999). This exploitative enterprise needed a set of truths about both the colonized and colonizer that legitimated the colonization process and the unequal treatment and access to resources that this would bring about. Particularly apparent in this period is the creation of pseudo-scientific hierarchies of race and the reliance (and subsequent perpetuation of) unfounded assumptions about 'othered' (non-Western/non-white) race underpinned many accepted approaches to social research (see Ratcliffe 2004): 'The premise that there are distinct races with biologically inherent characteristics or culturally immutable ethnicities has proved to be little more than a fabulous fiction, a myth of modernity' (Nayak 2006: 411).

The ideological tension in the history of the West as a despotic power, at the very moment of the birth of modern democracy and modernity, has been well noted (Said 1978; Spivak 1987). The West imagined the East according to its own needs (Said 1978; Fanon 1986). 'Colonial discourse' refers to the different strategies of description and understanding which were produced out of the historical emergence of this transnational network of power relations. Historically, distinct strands of colonial discourse circulating in particular colonial societies were linked to Western imperialist definitions of colonized populations (Fryer 1984; Malik 1996). Although there has been significant dismantling of this global political structure since the Second World War, neocolonial preoccupations continue to haunt Western perceptions of excolonial societies and their ethnic groups (Lawrence 1982). However, Western modernity's philosophical outlook steadfastly sanctioned a disavowal of ethnicity and affectively denied the role of ethnicity in framing knowledge in the modern period.

The postmodern and postcolonial perspective has been used by writers to force us to rethink the profound limitations of accepted and established knowledge about what civilization, rationality, progress, freedom and rights actually mean in liberal democracy, and how they can be understood as 'racialized'. It allows us to see that the consensual, collusive values paraded as universal and aspirational in the current globalized climate are not abstract but have a historical background; which is understood, known and located through the aegis and frameworks of Western rationalism and historicism. The race of different groups is not then interpreted in a vacuum but in a historical and contemporary framework. What constitutes a 'progressive race' or an 'acceptable race' is measured against the established norms of 'civility' and 'liberal democracy' that exist in Western societies.

Pause for reflection

It may be helpful at this point to think about some of the concepts commonly used in social research, such as objectivity, empiricism and trace their historical origins. There are some concepts like equality and social justice which are ringfenced or bracketed off from serious critique (Bonnett 1996: 878). What do they have in common (what do they exclude) and what do they tell us about the apparatuses for doing social research on race?

Foucault (1979b) has argued that part of the problem with modernity is that its framework for understanding the world, although critiqued, remains present in the majority of academic discourse. For Said (1978) this is symptomatic of the persistent Orient/Occident binary. For Foucault the persistence of certain types of knowledge is inextricably linked to the operation of power in society. The most powerful groups are most likely to have their version of knowledge legitimated and accepted as the most authentic knowledge. In short, the continued use of Western modern binaries and constructs of knowledge must still serve a purpose for powerful groups in society otherwise they would have been disregarded once discredited. Western standards and goals – rationality and individualism – are thereby used to evaluate the cultures and histories of non-Western societies (Ong 1999). This arises in what Gayatri Spivak (1987) calls the 'epistemic violence' of the discourses of the Other in imperialism and the creation of Orientalism. If race research is both constituted by and constitutive of modernity, then current scholarship on race must interrogate its own location within the formations of modern power.

The ideas explored above are important because they illuminate several persistent difficulties with Western ideas about race which stem from an Enlightenment heritage. First, they assume a white racial norm; second, they have a historical specificity which must be made explicit if we are to understand the (in)visibility of race; and, third, they highlight the legacy of power/knowledge dynamics that can be traced from modernity to the current climate. Pratt (1992) notes how even though Europeans may feel that they are innocently recording the outside world, their accounts are shot through with recurrent images which, in effect, end up producing 'the rest of the world for European readerships at particular points in Europe's expansionist trajectory' (1992: 5).

Smith argues (1998: 42) 'that what counts as Western research draws from an "archive" of knowledge and systems, rules and values which stretch beyond the boundaries of Western science to the system now referred to as the West'. Stuart Hall makes the point that the West is an idea or concept, a language for imagining a set of complex stories, ideas, historical events and social relationships. Hall argues that the concept of the West functions in ways which: (1) 'allow us' to characterize and classify societies into categories; (2) condense complex images of other societies through a *system of representation*; (3) provide a standard *model of comparison*; and (4) provide criteria of evaluation against which other societies can be ranked' (Hall 1992). This is how others become knowable in Western mindmaps.

A key limitation of the way in which modernity generated ways of knowing was its reliance on binaries. Derrida (1976) work has shown how binaries are crucial in the Western system of knowledge, hiding cultural diversity and concealing the power structures that preserve the hierarchical relations of difference. Those terms that are pre-eminent and invested with truth achieve that status by excluding and marginalizing what they are not. A good example of this binarism is the construction of racial difference that pervades our language and is constructed around opposites, such as rational (associated with white ethnicity) / irrational (associated with non-white ethnicity) and savage (associated with non-white ethnicity) / civilized (associated with white ethnicity), etc. By assembling the heterogeneous possibilities of meaning within language into fixed dichotomies, binarism reduces the potential of difference into polar opposites. This stasis of meaning regulates and disciplines the emergence of new identities. It is at this point, where the potentialities of meaning are fixed that the margin is established. But it is more than a simple boundary marking the outer limits of the centred term because it functions as a supplement, marking what the centre lacks but also what it needs in order to fully confirm its identity. It is then an integral though displaced part of the centre, defining it even in its non-identity. Binarism operates in the same way as splitting and projection: the centre expels its anxieties, contradictions and irrationalities onto the subordinate term, filling it with the antithesis of its own identity; the Other, in its very alienness, simply mirrors and represents what is deeply familiar to the centre, but projected outside of itself. Said (1978) characterizes the relationship between the colonizer and the colonized as one of implacable dependence. It is in the processes and representations of marginality that the violence, antagonisms and aversions which are at the core of the dominant discourses and identities become manifest – racism, homophobia, misogyny and class contempt are the products of this frontier (Mercer 1994; McClintock 1995). But it is in its nature as a supplement to the centre that the margin is also a place of resistance. The assertion of its existence threatens to deconstruct those forms of knowledge that constitute the subjectivities, discourses and institutions of the dominant, hegemonic formations. It is here, where power relations and historical forces have organized meaning into polar opposites that language becomes a site of struggle. Even as difference is pathologized and refused legitimacy, new terms and new identities are produced on the margins.

This collective memory of imperialism has been perpetuated through the ways in which knowledge about indigenous peoples was collected, classified and then represented in various ways back to the West, and then, through the eyes of the West, back to those who have been colonized. Edward Said (1978: 2) refers to this process as a Western discourse about the Other which is supported by 'institutions, vocabulary, scholarship, imagery, doctrines, even colonial bureaucracies and colonial styles'. According to Said, this process has worked partly because of the constant interchange between the scholarly and the imaginative construction of ideas about the Orient. The scholarly construction, he argues, is supported by a corporate institution which 'makes statements about it [the Orient], authorizing views of it, describing it, by teaching about it, settling it, ruling over it' (Said 1978: 3). It is strange in comparison to the West and more specifically whiteness.

In these acts both the formal scholarly pursuits of knowledge and the informal, imaginative, anecdotal constructions of the Other are intertwined with each other and with the activity of research. This book identifies research as a significant site of struggle between the interests and ways of knowing of the West and the interests and ways of resisting of the Other.

To put matters succinctly, modernity created a system of knowledge which must be understood in the context of the imperialist expansion stage of Western development. During this period understandings of progress, culture and civilization were all heavily eschewed in terms of inferiorizing non-Western cultures. Thus black and South Asian racial groups, for example, were misrepresented and measured against a specific but unacknowledged norm: the white, middle class male (Mani 1990). Moreover, given the Western power domination, their hold of knowledge meant that 'Othered' culture saw this knowledge as real and accepted it as a truthful representation of who they were. So what are the implications for the contemporary researcher and what ways forward have been forward by established researchers which can be utilized?

Strategies forward: Developing alternative concepts

There is scepticism as to whether tools of analysis developed in the modern Western framework of knowledge can ever be used to secure new, non-Western ethnocentric knowledge about marginalized groups in society:

> No sooner do we mention 'race' than we are caught in a treacherous bind. To say 'race' seems to imply that 'race' is real: but it also means that differentiation by race is racist and unjustifiable on scientific, theoretical, moral and political grounds. We find ourselves in a classic Nietzschean double bind: 'race' has been the history of an untruth, of an untruth that unfortunately [forms our] history ... The challenge here is to generate, from such a past and a present, a future where race will have been put to rest forever.
>
> (Radhakrishan 1996: 81)

For many there is an urgent need to not only expose the limitations of conventional ways of knowing by utilizing postmodern and postcolonial critiques but also to supersede them with alternative concepts and understandings (Said 1978; Mani 1990). For some there is very little option, given this framework, for a race researcher to break away from conventional frameworks of knowledge production which draw on this heritage and to go down alternative roads. As Audre Lorde ([1979] 1981: 98) famously wrote, albeit with special reference to gender, 'the master's tools will never dismantle the master's house'. For many contemporary researchers a prime way to circumvent these limitations is to create an alternative archive of knowledge from which theory and concepts can be developed.

Case study

A key way for doing this is planning a research project that allows 'raced' people to articulate themselves in their own terms, thereby securing a new archive of knowledge. Linda Tuhiwai Smith (1999) in her exploration of the intersections of imperialism, knowledge and research wishes to 'decolonize' research methods by writing from the perspective of the colonized. In 'setting an agenda for planning and implementing indigenous research' this author shows how such a programme can form part of a 'wider project of reclaiming control over indigenous ways of knowing and being' (1999: 3). She advocates situating the development of counterpractices of research within both Western critiques of Western knowledge and global indigenous movements.

Smith (1999: 42) argues

> from an indigenous perspective Western research is more than just research that is located in a positivist tradition. It is research which brings to bear, on any study of indigenous people, a cultural orientation, a set of values, a different conceptualization of such things as time, space and subjectivity, different and competing theories of knowledge, highly specialized forms of language, and structures of power
>
> (Smith 1999: 42)

What is at stake in doing 'indigenously focused' research is not just freeing us from Western constructs of doing research but freeing up indigenous people to think about themselves and have legitimacy. For a long time the East has imagined itself through the constructs of the West, creating a different basis on which to generate knowledge would help to change this.

Smith's (1999: 124) strategy for doing indigenous research

> Research is highly institutionalized through disciplines and fields of knowledge, through communities and interest groups of scholars, and through the academy. Research is also an integral part of political structures: governments fund research directly and indirectly through tertiary education, national science organizations, development programmes and policies . . . All of these research activities are carried out by people who in some form or another have been trained and socialized into ways of thinking, of defining and of making sense of the known and unknown

It seems rather difficult in this context to conceive of an articulation of an indigenous research agenda. A good start a researcher can make in trying to counterbalance this training is naming according to an indigenous world view, for example,

> what researchers may call methodology . . . Maori researchers in New Zealand call Kaupapa Maori research or Maori-centered research. This form of naming is about

bringing to the centre and privileging indigenous values, attitudes and practices rather than disguising them within Westernised labels such as 'collaborative research'.

(Smith 1999: 125)

There are two distinct pathways through which an indigenous research agenda can be advanced. 'The first one is through community action projects, local initiatives and nation or tribal research based around claims. The second pathway is through the spaces gained within institutions by indigenous research centers and studies programmes . . . the two pathways are not at odds with each other but simply reflect two distinct developments'. They intersect and inform each other at a number of different levels.

A practical step to implement Smith's strategy in your own research could be to start with an exploration of the history of knowledge of the raced community you are researching. Do they have a tradition of knowing that is different from the one you have been trained in? In what ways are your assumptions based on a history of contact between your two cultures? This may enable you to employ a culturally sensitive methodology, for example one that has an appreciation of oral history and the way knowledge is differently transferred in various cultures. For example Smith (1999) argues that greater legitimacy is given to written sources in the West, while Maori culture is more about oral narratives, which means that the most accessible material about Maoris was not written by Maori people, 'therefore, the potential to reproduce colonizing ideologies and colonizing perspectives is always present' (Smith 1999: 172). Kaupap Maori research – Maori centred research – should focus on research problems which are significant for the Maori. So when doing a literature search in preparation for a research project, non-Western formats should be sought. The point should be to generate a powerful body of counterknowledge that has as much gravitas as that of established knowledge. Smith's (1999: 163) agenda for indigenous research from her experience of researching the Maori people argues that the researcher should work with the community organizations, use language they are familiar with and make the most of the spaces opened up in the social sciences by more critical and reflexive approaches to research.

Modernity and empiricism

Part of the strategy advocated by theorists like Smith (1999) involves a rejection of positivism and empirical methodologies, as they are viewed as inevitably causing one to produce similar knowledge about race. Positivism championed the notion of research as an objective, value-free and scientific process for observing and making sense of human realities. The sustained critique of paradigms of knowledge that assumed unproblematic understandings of rationality, objectivity and neutrality in research has resulted in a widely accepted argument that objectivity is contested and should be considered of limited use in social science research (Ali 2006). All knowledge should be viewed as partial and situated. Researchers like Smith (1999) want 'raced' people to be at the heart of new research methods, which would focus on qualitative methods of inquiry including ethnography.

Alexander (2006: 400) writes that 'ethnography should be understood as the study of people in their own "natural" setting, with a focus on capturing and re-presenting the subjects' own understanding of their world'. While various methods and combination of methods can be employed, the research is centred on an extended period of fieldwork, with an emphasis on bottom–up generation of social meanings, categorizations and theorization (Brewer 2000; Alexander 2006; Wacquant 2007). As Malinowski (1922: 25) famously declared the aim is 'to grasp the native's view of the world'. The existence of the native view in recent years has been problematized with many writers dismissing it's existence (Asad 1973; Rosaldo 1989; Chow 1996). Ethnography is also different in different societies (for the distinction between British and American traditions, see Brewer 2000; Wacquant 2007).

The commitment to providing 'some kind of voice' (Willis and Trondman 2000) has been a source of criticism in researching race. In Britain, for instance, ethnography has been seen as a neocolonial process (Sharma et al. 1996), perpetuating an idea of difference and removal from broader structural debates. The most influential criticism of ethnography, as a mode of writing, can be found in the seminal volume *Writing Culture: The Poetics and Politics of Ethnography* (Marcus and Clifford 1986).

By contrast, there is a distinguished tradition of ethnographic studies in the US (from Whyte 1943 to Wacquant 2007) which has been respected and influential as a way of accessing, understanding and speaking for the marginalized and voiceless within American society. In America, as Alexander (2006: 401) notes, ethnographic studies have made a distinguished contribution to understanding America's racial landscape. From William Whyte's classic 1943 study of Italian Americans, *Street Corner Society*, through Elliot Liebow's (1967) timeless *Tally's Corner* and Elijah Anderson's ([1976] 2003) *A Place on the Corner* to contemporary studies such as Anderson's (1990) *Streetwise* and *The Code of the Street* (1999); Mitchell Duneier's (1992) *Slim's Table* and *Sidewalk* (1999); Sudhir Venkatesh's (2000) *American Project*; and Loic Wacquant's (2006) *Body and Soul*.

However, many contemporary ethnographers such as Trondman (2006) make clear, the practice and potentialities of ethnography are already dislocating traditional ways of understanding and writing 'race'. In Britain, for example a new generation of ethnographers have sought to reimagine the ethnography of 'race' through the contested and fragmented lense of the 'new ethnicities' framework (Alexander 1996, 2000; Back 1996; Kalra 2000; Alleyne 2002; Ali 2003; Nayak 2003). In the US, a new field of 'critical ethnography' has emerged within critical race studies, which places ethnography within a broader field of political struggle over racism and the relations of representation (Twine and Warren 2000).

Alternative sources

For theorists like Smith (1999) this indigenously focused research will transform communities' perception of themselves vis-à-vis research. Smith (1999: 44) argues that

> Western knowledges, philosophies and definitions of human nature form what Foucault has referred to as a cultural archive of histories, artefacts, ideas, texts and/or images, which are classified, preserved, arranged and represented back to the West. This store house contains the fragments, the regions and levels of knowledge traditions, and the 'systems' which allow different and differentiated forms of knowledge to be retrieved enunciated and represented in new contexts'.
>
> (drawn from Hall 1992)

Foucault suggests that the archive reveals 'rules of practice' which the West itself cannot necessarily describe because it operates within the rules and they are taken for granted. Various indigenous peoples would claim, indeed do claim, to be able to describe many of those rules of practice as they have been 'revealed' and/or perpetrated on indigenous communities. Hall has suggested that the Western cultural archive functions in ways which allow shifts and transformations to happen, quite radically at times, without the archive itself and the modes of classifications and systems of representations contained within it being destroyed. This sense of what the idea of the West represents is important here because to a large extent theories about research are underpinned by a cultural system of classification and representation, by views about human nature, human morality and virtue, by conceptions of space and time, by conceptions of gender and race. Ideas about these things help determine what counts as real. Systems of classification and representation enable different traditions or fragments of traditions to be retrieved and reformulated in different contexts as discourses, and then to be played out in systems of power and domination, with real material consequences for colonized peoples.

Pause for reflection

The following questions might help when thinking about contributing to an alternative archive knowledge:

- Whose research is it?
- Who owns it?
- Whose interests does it serve?
- Who will benefit from it?
- Who has designed its questions and framed its scope?
- Who will carry it out?
- Who will write it up?
- How will the results be disseminated?
- Has an ethnical accountability been established to those being researched?

Research on underexplored raced communities

Researchers seeking to challenge conventional methodological frameworks have also advocated the strategy of focusing on underexplored communities, such as white groups, or in the context of the United States, South Asians and Latinos, to complicate the black/white binary (Prashad 2000). Whiteness is frequently naturalized and left to stand as a deracialized (and also often a de-ethnicized) norm, with race being the defining property and experience of 'Other' groups. Dyer (1997), Fanon (1986), Frankenberg (1993), Goldberg (1993) and Mills (1997) among others have argued that a good way to challenge this set of assumptions is to study the implications of the privileged position of whiteness in race research.

Despite the obvious presence of the racial difference of the 'Other' in modernity paradigms, the whiteness of the dominant West was conspicuous by its absence. The lack of critical analysis is indicative of the motivation a colonial enterprise needed. The

Western world, as evidenced by theorists of this time, was in the embrace of Enlightenment ideals and was marked by the dominance of the East by the West. Fanon (1986), DuBois (1995) and more recently Dyer (1997) all point to the power of invisible whiteness, both in the West's historical and current stages of development, this is made explicit in the quote below:

> The dominant impulse of whiteness took shape around the notion of rationality or the European enlightenment, with its privileged construction of the transcendental white male rational subject ... in this context whiteness was naturalized as a universal entity that operated as more than a mere ethnic positionality emerging from a particular time, the late seventeenth and eighteenth centuries, and a particular space, western Europe.
>
> (Kincheloe and Steinberg 1998: 5)

Like all social categories, the boundaries of whiteness shift over time and place. What is revealed in the period after modernity, with the advent of the postmodern critique, is the fictional character of Western universality. The universal subject who arrogated the power to speak on behalf of humanity was nothing but a minority himself – the hegemonic white male bourgeois subject, whose centred identity depended on the Othering of subordinate class, racial, gendered and sexual subjects. The idea that 'whites' might themselves be important objects of consideration was by and large overlooked in mainstream writing until the 1990s. Traditionally race relations discourses have focused on the cultures of ethnic groups and patterns of discrimination as they affected black and South Asian ethnic groups. The process associated with globalization and postmodernity have fundamentally contributed to this shift in focus and it has in turn influenced our understanding of processes of racialization and forms of ethnic mobilization (Bhattacharyya et al. 2002). It is as important to understand the composition of racial privilege as it is to understand the composition of race through disadvantage. Many writers are concerned with whiteness, less in its extreme political manifestations and more with its role in securing privilege through seemingly neutral discourses. In the words of Nelson Rodriguez (1998: 50), 'whiteness is "so there everywhere" that we rarely question its spaces, logics, or assumptions'.

This continued privileging of whiteness, among other continuing patterns of modern inequality, has led to scepticism about the 'newness' of postmodernity.

Case study

White Women, Race Matters: The Social Construction of Whiteness (Frankenberg 1993) offers an ethnographic account of whiteness based upon both in an intimate relationship with the subject of study itself and upon indepth, life history interviews with 30 white women resident in the US. In it Frankenberg discusses the challenges that she faced while seeking to interview white women on a topic at times invisible and at other times 'taboo'. She found the following strategy of 'placing' whiteness in an analytical frame important in understanding it. 'First whiteness is a location of structural advantage, of race privilege. Second, it is a "standpoint", a place from which white people look at ourselves, at others and at society. Third, "whiteness" refers to a set of cultural practices that are usually unmarked and unnamed.' This theoretical conceptualization of whiteness was employed with recursivity, reflexivity and social constructionism by Frankenberg to research whiteness effectively.

The recognition of this discursive interlacing of social differences means that the 'majority/minority' binary, which is so prevalent in racial thinking, is disrupted (Brah 1996), so that whiteness is decentred as a 'pervasive normative presence' (Bonnett 1996: 97) as we come to understand it as a racial category, in other words as being socially located, internally differentiated and unstable.

A closely related epistemological break is engendered by an engagement with the concept of relationality, which concerns the erosion of a system of knowledge production and analysis based upon categorization, coherence and stability, and a move towards the recognition of a more contextual, contingent and ambivalent form of knowing. If we recognize that postcoloniality and related processes of globalization and multiculturalization are unsettling the traditional binary meanings of 'race' and ethnicity, and that these categories are always inscribed by multiple forms of difference, then categorization as we know it is disrupted. Research on 'race' and ethnicity must now develop analytical frameworks that are capable of addressing the relational and situated nature of identities, and their production, negotiation and contestation at the social and subjective levels.

What this means in relation to social research is that it is not enough to address the marginalizaton and the pathologization of minoritized experiences in research by simply focusing analytical attention upon these experiences, or by attending to the inadequacy of racial and ethnic categories in research by an obsessive expanding and refining of categories (Barker et al. 1994). Such processes can reverse processes of analytical marginalization, but they continue to constitute 'race and ethnicity through the same discursive systems, based upon fixed binary categorizations between a normalized whiteness and negatively valued, pathological or deviate 'Otherness'.

What is needed is a reflexive analytical doubleness. This doubleness entails being able to address the historical particularity and the plurality of racialized and ethnicized difference at the same time as interrupting binary systems of knowledge production. This is especially important in the age of superdiversity (Vertovec 2006).

Gunaratnam (2003: 22) has utilized Marcus's (1998) concept of multisited research as a device that offers potential to move beyond banal acknowledgement of relationality towards a focus upon specific, embodied practices and interrelations in research; towards details of how difference is produced and has effects within specific sites; and towards an examination of how these forms of difference might be connected across very different social spaces and experiences. This connects with the post-race critique discussed earlier in the volume about moving beyond ontological signifiers of race.

Strategies forward: Working subversively

The second group of strategies while accepting that there is a fundamental epistemological and methodological tension in the research of race in terms of what Radhakrishan (1996) has called the 'treacherous bind' advocate the possibility of working both with and against existing racialized categories and research approaches simultaneously.

As Hall (1996, 2000) notes, 'race' and related concepts such as ethnicity, identity, diaspora and multiculturalism – are so 'discursively entangled' (incapable of 'pure' meaning) that they can only be used 'under erasure'. Following Derrida (1981), Hall's reference to concepts operating 'under erasure' signals a deconstructive approach that recognizes our relation to concepts that have passed their analytical sell-by-date, that are no longer good to think with, but which have yet to be replaced.

For Hall (1996: 1), in the interval, 'there is nothing to do but to continue to think with them – albeit now in their detotalised or deconstructed forms, and no longer operating with the paradigm in which they were originally generated'. This involves recognizing race as a concept that operates 'under erasure', a concept that cannot be thought of in the 'old way' as representing essential, discrete differences between groups, but which we still need in order to address and dismantle racism. This understanding speaks to the dangerousness (the treacherous bind) of research on race evoked by Radhakrishan (1996).

Gunaratnam (2003: 23) building on this writes that what we need is a 'doubled' research practice that is capable of working both with and against racialized categories, and which is able to make links between lived experience, political relations and the production of knowledge.

Clearly it is not feasible to reject all theory and all research. One of the challenges for race researchers is to convince racialized people of the value of research for themselves, to convince researchers that greater research participant involvement is good, to develop approaches and ways of carrying out research which take into account, without being limited by, the legacies of previous research, and the parameters of both previous and current approaches. Some postcolonialist theorists, for example, have spoken about the need to be recognized within existing structures to be taken seriously. The position of postcolonial intellectuals is 'still highly problematic'. Gayatri Spivak (1990), who writes as a postcolonial Asian/Indian intellectual working in the United States, argues that Third World intellectuals have to position themselves strategically as intellectuals within the academy, the Third World or the indigenous world, and within the Western world where many intellectuals actually work. The problem for Third World intellectuals, she argues, remains the problem of being taken seriously. Accordingly she writes, 'For me, the question "Who should speak?" is less critical than "Who will listen?"' (Spivak 1990: 59–60). Indeed an appropriate response to racism from the perspectives of a number of influential writers such as Miles (1989) has been a careful critique of the concept of race and ethnicity.

A new generation of ethnographers, a number of whom come from minority communities, has been concerned with reclaiming and redefining the role of the ethnographic research. Contributions from Trondman (2006) and Rogilds (2006) make this clear: the practice and potentialities of ethnography are already dislocating traditional ways of understanding and writing 'race'.

In race and ethnic studies the question, 'How do we know what we think we know?' is much more than philosophical speculation. Indeed, it has become something of a prerequisite for ethnographers to consider the theory of knowledge and the relationship between forms of knowing, objects and experience. This *epistemological reflexivity* has paved the way for a series of blistering critiques concerning the ethics and politics of ethnographic enquiry (Nayak 2006: 412). This can be represented in the assumption one starts off with regarding ethnic groups, for example that Chica/nos have a gang culture, Asians have arranged marriages, etc. The methodological and practical issues discussed here have been particularly discussed with regard to representing otherness in race research, conducting ethnographical fieldwork.

Case study: Subversive ethnography

Alexander (2006: 405) writes that ethnography is perhaps one of the most controversial forms of research and writing on race, particularly in Britain. This is partly because of its historical underpinnings, 'but also the levels of intimacy and trust that ethnography both necessitates and questions [highlights] ... more general issues on how research can and should be conducted'. It is one of the most critically reflexive forms of research and writing (Clifford and Marcus 1986; Clifford 1988, 1997; Rosaldo 1989; Geertz 2000).

The debates on ethnography across national boundaries and disciplines are usefully summarized around the power inequalities in ethnographic production, its necessary partiality and its seemingly integral process of 'Othering' have both constrained ethnographic research on 'race' and inspired creative engagements with its forms. Alexander (2006: 402) argues, 'In Britain for example, a new generation of ethnographers have sought to reimagine the ethnography of "race" through the contested and fragmented lense of "new ethnicities" framework' (Alexander 1996, 2000; Back 1996; Kalra 2000; Alleyne 2002; Ali 2003; Nayak 2003). In the US, a new field of 'critical ethnography' has emerged within a broader field of political struggle over racism and the relations of representation (Twine and Warren 2000). Although there are differences in the histories and disciplinary practices of 'race' research in both places, the central, shared concerns of ethnographers of 'race' are on the negotiation and construction of 'difference' in 'the field' and in writing, the acknowledgement and partial amelioration of power hierarchies in the research process and the engagement with the broader local and global political contexts and realities of 'race'.

Nayak (2006: 413) writes 'A striking feature of early race ethnographies is that they are produced through and against a cultural standard of white normalcy. In turn this has led to pathological perceptions of racialized 'Others' as a problem, for example as 'deviant', 'caught between two cultures', 'in crisis', 'emasculated' or other such deficit explanations (see Taylor 1976; Watson 1977; Cashmore and Troyna 1982). It is 'now evident that modern day ethnographers are increasingly race conscious, reflexive and critically aware practitioners of this most subtle art of translation.

> We are now much better informed about the kaleidoscopic relations of power that permeate aspects of out research from initial design through to the write up, interpretation and reading of these narrative accounts. We are also more sensitive to the partiality of our stories, the complex configurations of power that underscore these relations, and the limits of representation as discursive practice
>
> (Nayak 2006: 413)

Postmodern theoretical standpoints

Postmodernism involves a shift from the non-reflective, passive level of acceptance and acquiescence to an active reflexivity and critique. The 'postmodern' frame as theorized by Rattansi (1994) draws upon a wide range of authors, for example Derrida (1976); Foucault (1979a); Giddens (1991); and Bauman (1991). An element of critical reflexivity by any researcher should act as a powerful counter balance to a simple recreation and perpetuation of an eschewed body of knowledge. In many ways although there is scepticism regarding the extent to which postmodern has created a space in which a new type of knowing can occur it is true that there are many ways in which a race research can use the critical frameworks developed here to understand the implications of the concepts and research they are doing. For many, postmodern frameworks can provide the tools for working subversively with existing paradigms and concepts in race research (Ali 2003; Ramji 2008).

Researchers are encouraged, using this critique, to think about how they are positioned. This challenge has focused on the notions of reflexivity and openness to challenge. Patti Lather (2001) has referred to this new grounded research as 'post-postivism', a term which comes out of poststructuralist and postmodern approaches to knowledge. The advice from this position is that you can work with concepts as a researcher as long as you are aware of what you are working with. It is useful here to draw on Sandra Harding's (1987: 2–3) very simple distinction between methodology and method, that is, 'A research methodology is a theory and analysis of how research does or should proceed ... [and] A research method is a technique for (or way of proceeding in) gathering evidence'. Methodology is important because it frames the questions being asked, determines the set of instruments and methods to be employed and shapes the analyses.

Feminist research has long argued for a radical reflexivity in research that involves rigorous attention to explicating the ways in which research participants and researchers are socially situated (Haraway 1988) at the same time as making our research accountable to the past (Gatens and Lloyd 1999). Related to this latter aspect of reflexivity is that researchers have to examine and trace how research is entangled with wider social and historical relations, and involves the ideological construction of the subject of its enquiry (Bauman 1991). For Gunaratnam (2003: 7) the idea that research is part of a social and historical relationship, which produces rather than simply reflects what we are researching, is encapsulated in the conceptualization of research as a *discursive practice*. Researchers should think how this might be part of what Levine (2000: 17) has called 'epistemology as political control'.

This allows us to challenge research as an unlocated and transparent reflection of some pre-existing, stable 'reality'. It makes our analyses more complex as the research task becomes one in which we need to make sense of knowledge as an emergent property of the interactions between and among differently constituted and located individuals – who include the researcher (Hemmings 2002). It also situates our knowledge claims in relation to historical and social relations. This is important if the researcher is to appreciate that race is a social construct. As several theorists have shown (Bonnett 1998; Gilroy 2000), there are close connections between the nature and aims of research concerned with questions of 'race' and ethnicity, and the social contexts in which race is conceptualized, developed and practiced.

Frankenberg (2004: 106) advocates a 'reflexive/recursive' approach to race research in her exploration of whiteness. Her own 'methods and analytical work as they have developed over two-plus decades reveals that not only method and analytical practice but also the content of the research and theorization are *themselves* "reflexive/recursive" in process, content and outcome'. She uses the term 'reflexive' to convey, that 'the positioned-ness of the researcher/theorist must be examined and accounted for ... [it] signals ... recognition of the impossibility of any Archimedean, objective, or "all-seeing" stance'. However,

> insisting that the place from which one undertakes research is as complex as the socio-cultural setting from which one sets out to document one's subject of study does not by itself account for one's perceiving capacity. For the researcher's perspective is also connected with a politicized, thinking consciousness such that one's mode of interpretation will be connected with communities of meaning in significant ways.
>
> Thus, one research practices will be amenable to formation and transformation in ways that are, perhaps, only fully explicable well after the fact of perception itself. Thus examining and accounting for one's positionedness is a difficult business, and the notion of recursive reading becomes critical to the interpretive journey.
>
> (Frankenberg 2004: 107)

This for her has always involved a strategy of revisiting any research conclusions and engagement where possible in longitudinal studies where repeat interviews over time are possible:

> I use the term 'recursive' to suggest that past conclusions are not necessarily closed. Rather they are potentially open to re-examination, and revision, and also available as resources for later research and theory. Thus, theoretical results can become the 'data' of future work. Conversely, data can be recognized subsequently as having already been positioned (more or less consciously from the standpoint of the author) and, hence, unconsciously theorized before the conscious theorization process ever began.
>
> (Frankenberg 2004: 107)

For example Frankenberg notes,

> as any researcher conceives her/his interviewee sample, she or he inevitably makes decisions about the boundaries of class, race, gender, region, etc, placed around her or his data set. Likewise as she or he designs her or his information gathering tools, she or he will perforce decide what to ask and by what means to do so. Simply stated, these basic processes are never transparent, never anything other than located, and as a result, directive as much as they are objective in intention and result. Subsequent revision, rethinking, or supplementation of one's beginning premises then potentially makes visible that which was taken as *a priori* at an earlier stage.
>
> (2004: 107)

This postmodern stance allows a researcher to break away from seeing methodological standpoints as they once were. For example, Frankenberg's position is markedly distinct from

> the conventional view of the ethnographer [as] a neutral observer, a traveler across cultural borders, and once safely returned, a translator of cultural truths. The notion of 'participant observation' carries with it a number of assumptions: first, the privileging of experience – of 'participating' as a means of discovering cultural truths; second, the primacy of the ethnographer's gaze in discerning and purveying these truths; third, of a regulated and limited engagement with 'the Other' under study within the clear boundaries of 'the field'
>
> (Alexander 2006: 139)

Researchers have utilized a concept of 'reflexivity' as a form of managing power relations in the research process. This involves recognition that there may be an unequal power relationship between the researcher and researched in the research process, more often than not one that favours the former. Foucault (1978) has convincingly presented the case that power and knowledge are intimately connected. Those most powerful will have their version of knowledge accepted as truth. The West's domination resulted in greater power to define knowledge. The struggle now is that with this recognition comes the need to open up spaces for alternative ways of knowing.

Yasmin Gunaratnam (2003: 1) argues that a central concern in researching race 'is how we produce knowledge about difference (and how what we know or claim to know) is caught up with specific histories and relations of power'. Many researchers have addressed the issues of power inequality in their race research and have formulated strategies that may help less experienced researchers. Ali (2003) and Ramji (2008) have both noted the power that respondents have in resisting and renegotiating meaning in the research relationship. Thus it is important to understand as a researcher the ways in which the respondent can exercise power, and indeed where they should be able to. They offer case studies of the difficulties of trying to create non-hierarchical research relationships. Ali (2003) and Song and Parker (1995) argue that it is a particularly protracted discussion for non-white researchers, trying to create non-hierarchical relationships. For example, researchers may frequently have to tell respondents more about their own racial backgrounds than they had thought important, and may have their own sense of identity challenged (also see Islam's (2000) study of Bangladeshis in LA). These issues are discussed in greater detail in Chapter 4.

Pause for reflection

What do you think are the dangers associated with researchers giving away information about themselves?

For those who do see postmodernism as new, its potential for novel explorations of marginal ethnicity is immense. Questioning the universal assumptions of modern knowledge has created an unprecedented milieu in which it was possible to critically engage with the foundations that framed everything from the questions asked and answers sought about minority cultures. In addition the postmodern climate validated the equal worth of alternative modes of knowledge. Thus black and South Asian communities had a space to not just advance more representative knowledge about themselves but to have that knowledge accepted. Although the postmodern turn has provided some powerful tools with which to expose the essentialism of Western modern paradigms, it itself is not an unproblematic paradigm.

It is important to acknowledge that the critical theories which are covered under the umbrella of late or post-modernity are also formulated in the same part of the world as their predecessors and it could also be asked how well placed are they to critique their own historical foundations and represent ethnic 'others'. Gidden's (1991: 35) position for example has been read as being resolutely rationalistic. For Bendle (2002: 10) it is essentially a retreat into a Cartesian view of the self that has been undermined.

Summary

Social science research is based upon ideas, beliefs and theories about the social world. Western forms of knowledge also draw on cultural ideas about the human 'self' and the relationship between the individual and the groups to which he or she may 'belong'. Smith (1999: 48) argues that 'Human nature, that is, the essential characteristics of an individual person, is an overarching concern of Western philosophy even though "human" and "nature" are also seen to be in opposition to each other'. Social research traditions 'have emerged from or been framed by debates relating to human nature. The separation between mind and body, the investing of a human person with a soul, a psyche and a consciousness, the distinction between sense and reason, definitions of human virtue and morality, are cultural constructs' (Smith 1999: 48). Smith argues from Aristotle and Plato to Descartes 'these ideas have been transformed as philosophers have incorporated new insights and discoveries, but the underlying categories have remained in place'. Gunaratnam (2003) among others has successfully shown how modern Western history built on these ideas in developing social science methodology for researching race.

> Colonialism and the idea of Europe, was a founding moment of racial categorization ('racialization') and of classifying and reducing ways of being to visible, embodied and hierarchically ordered forms of 'difference'. Contemporary approaches to research on race are marked by these colonial legacies that need to be examined, recognized, challenged and undermined.
>
> (2003: 8)

They form what Levine has called 'epistemology as political control' (2000: 17).

This chapter has articulated a theme that is encountered at all points in the research process, whether made explicit in other chapters or not, how we produce knowledge about 'race' and difference, and how what we know (or what we claim to know) is caught up with specific histories and relations of power. The most productive strategies seem to rely on the researcher developing a critical and theoretically informed approach, which draws on ideas and paradigms from a range of different standpoints including postmodernist, feminist, critical 'race' and postcolonial theory.

Further reading

Brewer, J. D. (2000) *Ethnography*. Maidenhead: Open University Press. This book discusses current controversies about ethnography, as well as providing guidelines for good practice.

Crang, M. and Cook, I. (2006) *Doing Ethnography*. London: Sage. This book is a useful practical guide for the first time ethnographer, covering both the main issues and methods.

Frankenberg, R. (1993) *White Women, Race Matters: The Social Construction of Whiteness*. London: Routledge.

Gunaratnam, Y. (2003) *Researching 'Race' and Ethnicity: Methods, Knowledge and Power*. London: Sage.

Silverman, D. (2004) *Doing Qualitative Research: A Practical Handbook*, 2nd edn. London: Sage. This volume covers ethnography as well as other qualitative approaches and offers hands on practical guide to all aspects of doing a qualitative project using a wide range of examples.

Smith, L. T. (1999) *Decolonising Methodologies: Research and Indigenous Peoples*. London: Zed Books and University of Otago Press.

Twine, F. W. (2000) Racial ideologies and racial methodologies, in F. W. Twine and J. W. Warren (eds), *Racing Research, Researching Race: Methodological Dilemmas in Critical Race Studies*. New York: New York University Press, 1–34.

Notes

1   Although the chapter looks at these processes separately it is important to note that they are not mutually exclusive. For example, many would argue that postmodernism and globalization are interdependent processes (Giddens 1991; Bauman 1991, 1999; Turner 1994). For these theorists and others, like Said (1978, 1999), it is changes in the global order (decolonization) and the processes associated with globalization, such as

technological advancement and mass migrations, that have made the 'postmodern condition' which is marked by a questioning of established understandings of ethnicity possible. It is also important to mention that there is no consensus about the terms 'modernity' and 'postmodernity', for example Giddens (1991) prefers to refer to post-modernity as late modernity. It is not necessary to go over these debates here, others have done so effectively elsewhere (Rattansi and Westwood 1994), but it is possible to work with broad agreements of what the common features of these concepts are.

2   It not the objective of this chapter to provide an overview of the well rehearsed debate about modernity.

3 Surveying race

There has been significant discussion and debate about race in survey research. This chapter will focus on key features of this with the aim of providing some guidance on the problems likely to be encountered in doing this type of research.[1] Surveys are an important tool in researching race. They are frequently used, for example, to measure attitudes to race and count the number of racial groups in different societies, as well as key social indicators for these groups. However, the perspective of postmodernity and the types of critiques discussed in the previous chapter have made quantitative methodology, such as surveys in the social sciences, less popular. Surveys are seen as operating with an essentialized, 'objective' conceptualization of race constituted by fixed qualities that individuals 'have' by virtue of biology and/or culture, which can be discovered as 'truth' using standardized questions and by manipulating tightly controlled research conditions. Race is assumed to have the same table meanings within groups. Surveys are also seen as operating with an idea of an objective social reality which has no place for the type of emotionality that race is likely to put forward which threaten the pursuit of truth. For critics race needs to be understood as socially created not fixed and the survey technique as a potential place of creation. They argue that the surveying of race, the counting of statistics about race, has to go hand in hand with interpreting the meaning of race and race groups at different times and with considering the changing definitions of race.[2] In this context, the race of both the researcher and researched become relevant aspects of the creation of race, because they will effect how the survey is conducted. At a methodological level the variability in the reporting of opinions according to the race of the interviewer undermines the standardizing, generalizing impulse of surveys. For critics there is an incompatibility between the aims of surveys and their assumptions of race. At an epistemological level the apparent defensiveness of the racialized research participant in disclosing their 'real' thoughts and feelings on 'racial topics' in interracial interviews suggests an important emotional and interactional dimension to race that has implications for the conceptualization of race as objective (largely demographic) categories. There is then, at a theoretical level, a debate over the understanding of race with which the survey technique operates which subsequently throws up the wrong kind of methodology for researching race.

Despite what its detractors may argue, survey based research continues to be hugely influential. Surveys are still an important part of any social scientist's repertoire, as advocated in their continued use not just in small scale research projects but also in large projects concerned with race by government agencies and charities. Indeed it could be argued that government and other similar organizations display a preference for this type of research. A particular strength of surveys is the generation of longitudinal data, for example the national census. Qualitative researchers cannot answer questions about trends or the prevalence of inequality across large populations that policy makers may want. Modood et al. (1997); Ahmad et al. (2003); Loury et al. (2005) all provide important illustrations of studies that use large scale survey data sets to research race. Demographic data can illuminate the relevance of particular social trends as well as contextualizing the processes, meanings and identities elucidated in qualitative analyses (e.g., Modood et al. 1997; Loury et al. 2005).

One major benefit of including large scale demographic data and qualitative analyses in the same study is that the epistemological approach can be consistent for both sets of data. The result of this is that the criticism of atheoretical empiricism, uninformed by social meaning, in quantitative data and of rich, meaningful, but socially decontextualized qualitative analyses are avoided. Instead there is the possibility of increasing understandings of trends, current socio-economic circumstances and social processes.

This chapter will give an overview of the main difficulties a race researcher may face when using the survey technique and possible ways of overcoming them. This chapter is not about discrediting survey and quantitative more generally by espousing the superiority of qualitative approaches. Rather its interest is in exposing and facing up to the political nature of knowledge production (Gill 1998) which confronts both quantitative and qualitative research on race. Indeed this chapter is sympathetic to arguments that the distinction between qualitative and quantitative methodology is blurred and not absolute (Gunaratnam 2003; Payne and Grew 2005; Crompton 2008).

Pause for reflection

A survey when done well is an excellent information gathering tool. For example, what methods other than the survey could provide the information generated by the national census in different countries?

Histories and race surveys

First, you need to decide whether surveys are an appropriate tool for gathering the data for the research question you have set yourself. This will involve an interrogation of the issues discussed in the previous two chapters: specifically, what is your focus and what is the history around it?

For example, a difficulty is that surveys have histories with raced communities which may mean that they may not wish to participate in a research project despite being part of a sample. Surveys are frequently the source of data used to argue that race is a problem, for example that most muggers are black, and thus are accused of peddling stereotypes. Moreover, while historical survey research in a context of colonialism can be understood as marked by practices based upon the differentiation and control of racialized bodies (Levine 2000), more contemporary research can be seen as being characterized by political concerns about questions of cultural and national identity and belonging (Hall 1993). Hesse (2000: 11–12), in a discussion of contemporary postcolonial and multicultural relations, has identified a ubiquitous 'race relations narrative', which struggles with conflicting needs to monitor, control and assimilate racialized difference as being central to forms of governance. This need to monitor, with the hope of controlling and managing 'race relations', creates a real tension in contemporary research on 'race', and presents significant political dilemmas for researchers with regard to the relationships between policy agenda, research questions, methodological practices and the funding of research.

Case study

In a historical analysis of the development of surveys on 'minority' groups, Smith (1993) has shown how growing attention to 'race' in surveys, and particularly within opinion poll research in the US, was related to the need for more information on the opinions and beliefs of African American people as a result of civil rights activism. Before the 1950s, Smith argues, African American people were virtually invisible in survey research in the US, with such issues as the legal and illegal exclusion of African American people from voter registration records, preventing their participation in many opinion polls. It was only with the civil rights movement, and increasingly frequent debates about race equality, that the need for more information on African American people's opinion was recognized. Indeed, Stanfield (1993) has described the 1950s and 1960s as a 'heady time' for research on 'race relations', when 'there was a flood of federal and private foundation dollars for doing policy-related research' because of public concerns about desegregation and the civil rights movement (e.g., Shosteck 1977).

Strategies to limit non-response rates in surveys

Methods of data collection

The desired 80 percent response rate is becoming increasingly difficult for social surveys to achieve (Savage and Burrows 2007). As Fowler (2002: 58) notes, the choice of data collection mode (in surveys) – whether this is by mail, Internet, telephone, personal interview or group administration – is related directly to the sample frame, research topic, characteristics of sample and the availability of facilities. Each choice has implications for response rates, question form and survey costs. An inventory of the various considerations in and consequences of the choice of a data collection mode is presented well in Fowler's (2002) volume.

Pause for reflection

Should an interviewer ask the questions and record the answers, or should the survey be self-administered?

If an interviewer is to be used, there is the further decision about whether the interview will take place in person or over the telephone. If respondents are to read and answer questions without an interviewer, there are choices about how to present the questionnaire to the respondents. In some cases, questionnaires are handed to respondents, in groups or individually, and returned in a similar fashion. For those with Internet access, questions can be embedded in emails or respondents can be asked to go to a website to answer questions.

Although the majority of surveys utilize a single data collection method, it is not uncommon for combinations of methods to be used. For example, personal interview surveys sometimes have series of questions that respondents answer by filling out a self-administered form or entering answers directly into a laptop computer.

Fowler (2002: 59) argues that the way a researcher plans to draw a sample is related to considerations of the best way to collect data. Certain kinds of sampling approaches make it easy or difficult to use one or another data collection strategy. If one is sampling from a list, the information on the list matters. Obviously, if a list lacks accurate mailing addresses, email addresses or telephone numbers, trying to collect data by the corresponding mode is complicated.

As a student, sample listings that include email addresses obviously open that avenue for data collection. While email is not yet a practical option for general population surveys, there are many populations (employees, students, members of professional organizations) for which email addresses are nearly universally available and are easily available. In those cases, using the Internet as the main, or at least one, data collection mode may be a good idea.

Self-administered surveys place more of a burden on the reading and writing skills of the respondents. This presents difficulties as racialized communities are among the least well educated, and their reading and writing (but not necessarily spoken) skills in English are limited.

One of the best ways to minimize survey non-response is to use more than one mode to collect data. The key issues, as noted, are access, motivation and cost. Mixing modes can enable researchers to reach people who are inaccessible via a single mode. It also can allow them to collect data from less intrinsically motivated sample members. For example, one attractive protocol is to use email or mail for the first phase of data collection, followed by telephone interviews with respondents. Combining telephone and in-person interviews is another effective design. Dillman (2000) and Fowler (2002) provide good accounts of increasingly good response rates to self-administered surveys, including postal and Internet.

Case study: *The British Chinese Online. Collective Identity and Political Mobilisation* (Song 2004)

The Internet is defined variously as a communication medium, a global network of connections, and a scene of social construction. The shape and nature of Internet communication is defined in context, negotiated by users that may adapt hardware and software to suit their individual or community needs. Internet communication affords qualitative researchers creative potential because of it geographical dispersion, multimodality and chronomalleability. The researcher's own conceptualization of the Internet will influence how it is woven into the research project, with significant consequences on the outcomes. As social life becomes more saturated with Internet based media for communication, researchers will be able to creatively design projects that utilize these media to observe culture, interact with participants or collect artefacts. Each new technology has a double edge for researchers and users: as it highlights or enables certain aspects and qualities of interaction, it hides and constrains others. There has been a great deal of literature produced dealing with using the Internet in social research. Mann and Stewart (2000) provide an excellent methodological and ethical review of the Internet as a tool in social research. Among the advantages it provides for a race researcher are that it provides an excellent way of studying a globally dispersed group. It also enables cross-cultural comparisons, as it collapses time as well as distance. However, a major disadvantage is that since non-white groups are among the poorest in society their access to the Internet could be limited, creating problems for any survey conducted using this method. Among the pragmatic advantages of conducting a survey on race in this way is that it solves the issues of venue, travel and scheduling conflicts.

For Song (2004) a key difficulty was the problem of anonymity and authenticity of responses she received from the Chinese community she was researching online. As she could not verify the characteristics of people she relied on the information provided and the accuracy of their answers. In addition, the survey prompted sideline discussions and, because of the multimodal features of the Internet, multiple conversations could happen at the same time, adding depth but also difficulties for the researcher in keeping track of who was saying what. Another difficulty Song found was relating to the ethical concerns of accessing this community online for survey research. Although, you obtain permission to research these groups – and provide them with all the relevant information regarding the research project – there is still a difficulty in deciding which information is yours to use and which is private. Although many online discussion groups appear to be public, members may perceive their interaction to be private and can be surprised or angered by intruding researchers (Bromseth 2002). Other groups know that their communication is public but they nonetheless do not want to be studied (Gajjala 2002; Hudson and Bruckman 2002). For a good overview on ethnical problems of Internet research, see Frankel and Siang (1999) and Mann and Stewart (2000).

Song (2004) also found the control over the communication process a particular difficulty in conducting online research on the Chinese community. In particular, the complex combination of oral and written styles, the choice granted by anonymous software to create alternative identities online, and the ability to stop time (and the opportunity to reflect on and revise statements, not possible in spoken responses to surveys). These features gave greater control to respondents with regard to the content and form of the message, the presentation of self and over others' perception of the self.

However, it could be that these features contributed to a good and truthful range of responses. While many argue that rapport is needed in survey research, interestingly some findings suggest otherwise. Fowler (2002: 64), for example, argues that data clearly indicate that sensitive information is more frequently, and almost certainly more accurately, reported in self-administered modes than when interviewers ask questions. Both self-administered paper forms and computer assisted self-administration have been shown to produce the same results in comparison to interviewer administered protocols (Dillman 1991; Aquilino 1994; Turner et al. 1996; Tourangeau and Smith 1998). Moreover these results apply to very sensitive material.

One of the advantages of computer assisted personal interviewing (CAPI) is ease of question management and rapid compilation of data. Although still evolving, there are some additional interesting potentials that are likely to be realized. For example, computers make it possible to present information and stimuli in forms other than words (e.g., pictures). Computers have the potential to adjust the language of the questions to the language of the respondent, as well as to have questions read out loud for those who have difficulty reading. The possibility with computers for respondents to alter the choice or sequence of questions to fit previous answers is a particular strength in self-administration, where complex skip instructions are difficult for them. Call-in computers can ask questions and record answers via touchtone entry, offering an alternative to the Internet, and allowing respondents to provide data at any time they choose. Finally, respondents appear to be more comfortable keying sensitive information into computers than providing the same information to an interviewer.

For a comprehensive but succinct comparison of methods for collection data via a survey method, see Fowler (2002: 71–4).

Surveys

As Fowler notes 'the purpose of the survey is to produce statistics, that is, quantitative or numerical descriptions about some aspects of the study population' (2002: 1–2).[3] The main way of collecting information is by asking people questions: their answers constitute the data to be analysed.

Governments are the largest collectors of survey data, with information collected on everything from the health, to unemployment, and to criminal activity.

The census is a good example of a survey. It is a measure of 'the population to be governed and put to work, its housing, its employment, its level of education and training, and so on' (Sapsford 1999: 2).

Census

The British Census has taken place every 10 years since 1801, except for 1941, and aims to provide a complete count of every person resident in England and Wales (there are separate censuses of Scotland and Northern Ireland) and of the households or institutions within which they live. The Census of the Population in the United States is even older, having been held every 10 years since 1790, and the first Swedish Census also dates from the late eighteenth century

(Sapsford 1999: 2–3)

As Fowler (2002) notes there is probably no area of public policy to which survey research methodology has not been applied. In the US context he notes that unemployment, people's income and expenditure, health and crime are all subject to regular surveys.

What is a good survey?

Fowler (2002: 3) notes that what makes a good survey are 'good samples, good response rates, good questions, good interviewing and good data collection protocols. For all of these affect the quality of survey data'. Each one of these aspects has been critiqued from a race research perspective.

Pause for reflection

Three things are necessary, in a successful survey questionnaire:

- Clear, unambiguous questions – which are effective as indicators of a more complex concept, valid and reliable measures – to eliminate errors of measurement which might confuse the results.
- Standardization of presentation, so that everyone is asked precisely the same questions in the same order and as much as possible of the variation due to interviewer 'style' is eliminated.
- A trustworthy, efficient and, preferably, cost effective way of translating (coding) the data for subsequent analysis.

Sample

Generally, information is collected on only a fraction of the population, that is, a sample, rather than from every member of the population.

The census is unique in that it surveys every member of the population. Most surveys rely on a sample. Good examples of these include the Labour Market Survey and the British Household Panel. Sapsford (1999: 6) notes,

> A *sample* is a subset of the population – usually with the implication that the subset resembles the population closely on key characteristics (is *representative* of the population). If the sample is representative of the population, then what is true of the sample will also be true of the population (within a calculable margin of error), allowing valid generalizations to be made about the population on the basis of the sample. How well a sample represents a population depends on the sample frame, the sample size, and the specific design of selection procedures. The sample frame is the set of people that has a chance to be selected. Statistically speaking, a sample can be representative only of the population included in the sample frame. One design issue is how well the sample frame corresponds to the population a researcher wants to describe.

Pause for reflection

- There has been a great deal of interest in whether different races are neglected in sampling. For example, does some portion of the racialized population stand less chance of being selected?

- There are various difficulties that you may encounter, for example you may wish to concentrate your research on a particular racial minority exclusively, how do you get this sample? Or you may want to ensure a racially representative sample, to collect data from a cross-range of a racially diverse population, how do you go about getting this sample?

There are various ways a race researcher can go about finding solutions and these lie in understanding the various aspects of the sample selection procedure; the frame, size and selection procedures.

Problems with samples

All survey samples are sought to be representative but there are different techniques employed for achieving this.

Random sampling for example, selects cases at random, 'so that pure chance determines who is approached and every case has an equal chance of being selected this maximizes the likelihood that there will be no systematic bias in the sampling' (Sapsford 1999: 8). Fowler further argues that probability sampling enables one to have confidence that the sample is not a biased one. However, a probability sample selected from a non-vetted frame would not ensure racial representativeness. Similarly, random sampling does not produce a meaningful racial sample. The Millennium Cohort Study, for example, had to oversample South Asians in the UK in order to ensure that it had a sufficient quantity to analyse.

To have a probability or random sample of ethnic minorities in the UK the researcher needs a sampling frame that included enough of the population that you want to study. As no sampling frame exists in the UK for racial minorities there is reliance in most race research on non-random snowball samples. Many research projects do not have the privilege of a complete and accurate sampling frame, Sapsford (1999: 81) suggest ways we can make do.

Thus from the outset there is an understanding that because of the very nature of constructing a sample of minority non-white groups the personal bias of the researcher might enter the research process.

Strategies for sampling

Some researchers have created their own sampling frame by multiple approaches to the recruitment of the desired community to reflect its diversity. For example, to get a sample frame from which to select raced people, researchers have often used community organizations. Further the identification and selection of racialized minorities researchers advocate should be carried out in partnership with community organizations and community researchers (Islam 2000). This can secure a frame in which a sample can be found. The researcher then can decide whether to survey everyone the researcher has in their frame or to employ a sample selection technique.

Case study

Fowler (2002) demonstrates the importance of studying national demographical statistics in creating a sampling frame for researching race. Even if individual members of a subgroup of interest cannot be identified with certainty in advance of sampling, sometimes the basic approach outlined here can be applied. For instance, it is most unusual to have a list of housing units that identifies the race of occupants in advance of contact. It is not uncommon, however, for Asian, black or Latino families to be more concentrated in some neighbourhood areas than others. In that instance, a researcher may be able to sample households in areas that are predominantly Asian, for instance, at a higher than average rate to increase the number of Asian respondents. Savage and Burrows (2007) have recently argued that postcodes give as much sociological information about people that we need (Webber and Butler 2006; Burrows and Gane 2006). Probability sampling could be used once such a framework has been identified. The foundation of probability sampling (favoured by governments and academics) is that the inclusion of someone in a sample is based on a predetermined procedure that sets a rate of selection for members of a defined population. Beyond that, neither respondents' characteristics nor interviewer discretion influences the likehood that a person will be in a sample. Although non-probability modifications of sampling vary (preferred by public opinion polling groups), they all share the property that, at the last stage, interviewer discretion and/or respondent characteristics not part of the sample design affect the likelihood of being included in a sample.

Multistage sampling has also been usefully employed by race researchers. Fowler advocates this approach when there is no adequate list of desired individuals in a population and no way to get at the population directly. Fowler (2002) provides an extensive discussion about the sampling techniques that are on offer to researchers, including random sampling, systematic samples, stratified sample (see Fowler 2002: 15). Snowballing has been the most frequently used sample selection technique. Usually by creating sample frames from multiple community contacts. Also quota sampling is employed, where the choice of respondents is left up to the interviewers but with set constraints on their choice so that the sample matches the population desired.

Standardization and validity

As Sapsford (1999: 9) notes standardization lies at the heart of survey research, and the whole point is to get consistent answers to consistent questions. In answering what differentiates surveys from other kinds of research project, Sapsford (1999: 4) writes 'Surveys involve *systematic* observation or systematic interviewing. They ask the questions which the *researcher* wants answered, and often they dictate the range of answers that may be given'.

More than this, surveys try to ask the questions in precisely the same way in each instance – to *standardize* the questionnaire as a measuring instrument. It is upon this that the validity of surveys is based. Another important part of survey design is showing that your measurements are accurate and trustworthy (*reliable*) – that someone else using the same measurement tools would have obtained the same or similar results.

A variable is a measured quantity and surveys utilize the divisions among them. Descriptive variables are those which are just to be reported on, with no conclusions drawn about influence or causality; dependent variables are those we want to say are caused or influenced by others; independent variables are those we want to say are doing the causing or influencing; extraneous variables are those which, it might be argued, could provide an alternative causal explanation and so cast doubt on the explanation we are advancing. (For more details on levels of measurement including nominal, ordinal, integral or ratio scales, see Sapsford 1999).

Question design

For Fowler (2002: 5) using questions as measures is another essential part of the survey process. Good questions are reliable (providing consistent measures in comparable situations) and valid (answers correspond to what they are intended to measure). Fowler (2002: 105) further notes the 'survey instrument has two components: deciding what to measure and designing and testing questions that will be good measures. The first step usually is to define the survey objectives, though those objectives may be revised based on subsequent question testing'. The key is to write standardized questions for measuring subjective phenomena.

With surveying for race there is the problem of operationalization – getting from our concept of a characteristic worth measuring to something which can actually be measured; and validation – showing that the measures we have taken are indeed appropriate for the concept under discussion.

Operationalization requires the substitution of something the measurement of which a theory or hypothesis demands, by something which can actually be counted without ambiguity. Given an operationalized measure, the other logical necessity if it is to be used as evidence is validation – demonstrating that it does indeed measure what it purports to measure and has some claims to consistency and accuracy.

Pause for reflection

If survey methods don't operationalize 'race' properly how can they collect information about it?

The problem of operationalization

The difficultly for race researchers is that the operationalization of race changes in varying social contexts and interactions. Surveys are valued because they use the standardized questions and categories where the validity of the answers can be tested or verified using rigorous repetition. However there is serious debate regarding the extent to which these categories are abstract and removed from the context in which they are created.

There was considerable debate preceding the 1991 census in the UK, for example, which was the first British census to ask a question about ethnicity. Researchers such as Ahmad and Sheldon (1991, 1993) argued that the process of operationalizing ethnicity into distinct categories for the census was a reductionist political process, implying: 'The acceptance of some notion of homogeneity of condition, culture, attitudes, expectation and in some cases language and religion within the groups identified on an ethnic basis' (Ahmad and Sheldon 1991). Despite the categories in the 1991 census conflating a number of different elements, such as culture, geography, nationality and skin colour, the ethnicity data from the census has since been used in examining and challenging inequalities, particularly in public services (see Dyson 2001). For instance, Simpson (1997) has suggested that the demographic data from the 1991 census was critical in developing schooling policy. Categories have changed as the social meaning given to different races has been transformed, for example the fragmentation of the 'black' category into the various forms of identification available in contemporary censuses and, significantly, the introduction of religion in 2001.

With regard to the new question on religion asked in the 2001 census, Aspinall (2001) has argued that it allows for more complex data to be used. It has demonstrated differentials in the South Asian grouping, for example, indicating that this group is as differentiated among itself as it is from others.

Information generated through tightly defined categories of ethnicity and race, such as the census data, has been used in challenging forms of racialized inequality. But categories can be far from benign descriptors. Categories can also serve to construct racialized identifications, experiences, forms of governance and the meanings of social inequalities. For example, the census's religion question needs to be seen in the context of the rising significance of faith communities and discrimination based on religion (Richardson 1999).

There is a tension between the need to work with highly defined categories of race and the recognition that such categories are socially and historically contingent (for a debate about ethnic categories in research, see Modood et al. 2002 and Smith 2002).

Case study

Sophie Body-Gendrot and Duprez's (2002: 150) experience of race research in America and France makes this apparent. During the 1980s, they argue (2002: 152),

> Three elements made international comparisons on this topic most difficult at the time: the official ignorance of ethnic and racial discrimination that French citizens of postcolonial origin experienced and the lack of statistics concerning race and ethnicity; the amnesia relative to the Algerian War, unlike the awareness of the legacy of the slavery in the USA; the refusal of incorporating into cross national analyses 'the Trojan horse' embodied by the USA and the illegitimacy of comparing two vastly different societies

Among the difficulties French researchers face in doing international comparison on race and racism is defining race: 'Terms that appear similar to *race* do in fact in each country cover different histories and structures, they belong to diverse semantic spaces and traditions, and they cannot be translated as if they were alike'.

In the previous chapter we saw that there is a danger that by using categories without interrogating them researchers, however unintentionally, reify 'race' as 'entities that individuals are born in to and inhabit, and that are then brought to life in the social world, rather than recognizing race as dynamic and emergent processes of being and becoming' (Gunaratnam 2003: 19). Radhakrishan (1996) has described the 'treacherous bind' that exists in race research. 'The "treacherous bind" names and describes the dangerousness and the contradictions of our continued use and reliance upon racial and ethnic categories that can be complicit with racial typologies and thinking' (Gunaratnam 2003: 23).

Case study: *Stability and Change in Ethnic Groups in England and Wales* (Platt et al. 2005)

This study uses the census longitudinal survey to examine the impact of the changes in ethnic classification between the census of 1991 and 2001. For example, almost one in four persons reported as black Caribbean or black African in the 1991 census were reported in another category in 2001. Analyses of this survey data set tend to assume certain stability in the meaning of the ethnic group being studied: the insights into ethnic group differentiation are premised on the fact that the group has the same meaning over time. However Platt et al. (2005) show how the census longitudinal survey allows us to challenge such notions of group stability. This has practical implications of the ways we measure and conceive of Britain's minority ethnic groups. They illustrate this point by exploring the change in ethnic group identification by the same individuals between 1991 and 2001. They also provide some suggestions on the implications of this ethnic group instability for other research.

The longitudinal study is of a 1 percent sample of the population of England and Wales that is followed over time. It started in 1974. The first ethnic group question was asked in 1991 when 7 percent of the population described themselves as belonging to an ethnic group. In 2001, the ethnic group question was revised to reflect evolution in the terminology used to describe groups in England and Wales, and 9 percent of the population identified themselves as belonging to an ethnic group. The 2001 questions differed from the 1991 questions both in wording and in range of categories. These different categories enabled new options for self-identification and the opportunity for individuals to change their choice of group, for example the option of being Irish or having 'mixed' ethnic origins.

In addition, the census questionnaires of 1991 and 2001 gave different guidance notes to aid respondents in understanding what is meant by their 'ethnic group'. In 2001 respondents were asked to tick or write in their 'cultural background', while in 1991 the note used the term 'descended' and 'ancestry', giving more emphasis to family rather than to cultural origins.

Among those with an imputed ethnicity in 2001, less than half had been imputed with the same ethnicity when they had responded in 1991. This means that the composition of the groups with the same label at both censuses may not be directly comparable.

One practical implication of these findings is regarding how to treat ethnic group categories in a way that responds to group differences relating to issues of consistency in the responses in the 1991 and 2001 ethnic group questions. There are several possibilities for ensuring maximum stability when making comparisons between groups based on the 1991 and the 2001 classifications. Since changes in ethnic group identification are proportionately higher for some ethnic groups than for others, with for example white, Chinese and South Asian groups exhibiting strong stability, one solution is to amalgamate the most unstable 2001 groups into one diverse group. They base this new group on isolating the groups where less than half of a 2001 group originated from a single 1991 group (white and black Carribean, white and black African, white and Asian, and Other mixed). This classification maximizes the fit between the two measurement points, retains meaningful groups for analysis and ensures that conceptually the groups contain roughly the same sets of people at both points.

Pause for reflection

A statement of purposes, a list of the kinds of variables to be measured and a draft of an analysis plan are essential components for developing a survey instrument. However, even if the survey remains the same the following will change the results the survey will produce:

1   When questions are asked.
2   In what order.
3   To whom/by whom.
4   Responses may change over time – so in a longitudinal study how do you know the 'true' answer?

Strategies for operationalization

Pilot testing

Pretesting questions to find out if they are well understood and if the answers are meaningful is a useful technique to employ in surveying for race.

A good way to do this is to hold focus group discussion with the people who are in the study population. The primary purpose of these discussions is to compare the reality about which respondents will be answering questions with the abstract concepts embedded in the study objectives. Focus group discussions are best with six to eight participants. The general protocol is to discuss people's perceptions, experiences and, perhaps, feelings related to what is to be measured in the survey. For example, Wieviorka (2004: 55) in his work on researching race in France 'spent a lot of time preparing myself intellectually, constructing my analytical categories, week after week, during an annual seminar that led to a theoretical book. This effort was completed with the organization of a large intellectual colloquium on racism'.

Another strategy race researchers have found useful is to consult question banks. Many questions, such as those dealing with background or demographic issues, are standard to many surveys. Researchers, for example, have found reviewing questions in the General Social Survey carried out by the National Opinion Research Centre at the University of Chicago useful. Many surveys are also available online through the Inter-University Consortium of Political and Social Research (ICPSR) at the University of Michigan. Copies of original survey instruments from any of the major survey organizations are useful as references. Obviously there will be restrictions because some have a limited appreciation of race, or simply because debates have moved on. There is a wealth of information which is already available and it is useful to know how to use it. Importantly, there would be no point, except as a practice exercise, in carrying out a survey which has already been done by someone else. As Sapsford (1999: 233) writes, while replication is valuable, for example repeating someone else's research and obtaining the same answer gives you more confidence in the results, we do not carry out replication just for its own sake. Normally there has to be some special interest in the findings – for instance that they are implausible or counterintuitive on the face of it or a very important and/or costly decision depends on the results. It is important to consult the wide range of information that exists already, in libraries or in other places, to serve as evidence for the research or policy questions you want to ask. You should draw on this anyway to broaden the scope of your discussion. It may not be perfect, but it may be based on a larger sample or better resources. Libraries in various countries also have their own resources, for example BIDS (Bath Information Data Service), the online equivalent of the Social Science Citations Index has been found to be useful. From these, the researcher can glean ideas about how specific questions are phrased, how to generate standardized questions and how to format survey instruments. As Fowler (2002: 107) notes, taking advantage of the work that others have done is very sensible. Of course, it is best to review questions asked by researchers who have done previous work on the study topic, but be cautious. Bad questions may be included and used over and over again. All questions should be tested to make sure that they 'work' for the populations, context and goal of a particular study.

Figures taken from libraries or archives have, as with figures you collect yourself, to be subjected to validity checks. It is not enough to say, 'the government's figures show a rise in racism'. You need to examine how the figures were collected, from whom and under what circumstances, and to look carefully at the questions that were asked, the observations that were made or the incidents that were counted. That is, you need to satisfy yourself that the figures provide valid evidence for the conclusions you want to draw. Where this could be in doubt, you may also need to satisfy the reader or to explain what the limitations are on what can be concluded. For example, if there is to be a comparison with outside figures you always need to check beforehand how they are coded and presented, or to collect maximal detail (exact ages, exact incomes) and degrade into categories later. In Britain a useful book to consult is *Harmonised Concepts and Questions for Government Social Surveys* (Governments Statistical Service 1996), which sets out the form of questions agreed between government departments for common use.

Embracing reflexivity

It seems clear that to assume surveys can provide and produce objective knowledge is not feasible. However, if the researcher recognizes this using the tool of reflexivity discussed in the earlier chapter, then the survey can be a powerful methodological tool. The researcher in constructing/compiling a survey, or indeed in using survey findings, needs to recognize that he or she as a researcher are not removed from the object of their study.

Surveys are seen to be grounded in rationalist, emotion stripping approaches to researching 'race' characterized by positivist ideas about 'the disinterested observer seeking objective truth with universal validity that is based on the notion of a reality independent of human thought and action' (Huber 1995: 204). Race is frequently seen as getting in the way of discovering the truth. These rationalist approaches have been coming under criticism for their failure to address the irrational, unconscious and emotional dimensions of inter/subjectivity in research. For example, standardization is a way of eliminating emotion from the research process. Holstein and Gubrium (1998) have captured many of the methodological characteristics of survey interviews in their observation that:

> The interview conversation is ... framed as a potential source of bias, error, misunderstanding or misdirection, a persistent set of problems to be controlled. The corrective is simple; if the interview asks questions properly, the respondent will give out the desired information ... there is a highly sophisticated technology that informs researchers how to ask questions, what sorts of questions not to ask, the order in which to ask them, and the ways to avoid saying things that might spoil, contaminate or otherwise bias the data.
>
> (1998: 113–15)

Although statistics are often revered as providing 'hard facts', and as such are used by governments and public bodies as a basis for policy decisions regarding racial minorities and racism, they are not necessarily accurate indicators of the extent or character of race and racism. Two important limitations are: first, what they leave out both in terms of topics and people and, second, the problem of bias, the topics/questions and people surveyed may not be reflective of the wider population, that is a representation sample, but may say more about the researcher (and their social positioning) than the survey.

Race in many ways problematizes the framework of 'knowledge' that surveys are operating with, for instance by accepting that race is produced in an emotive interaction in surveys – you are questioning the foundation of survey research. Surveys are in fact not neutral tools of information collection. The conceptualization of racialized research participants as concealing their 'true' opinions about 'racial topics' posits a certain kind of 'research subject', raising questions about how racialized subjectivity is defined and what assumptions are implied. It is a research subject who is assumed to be a racialized un/consciousness and who is assumed to be deeply threatened by racialized difference. It is a research subject who is anxious and emotional and whose responses therefore cannot be trusted. The researcher in this equation is seen as objective, and more importantly he or she is not racialized – operating with an assumed whiteness or race neutral perspective.

Despite the standardizing drive of surveys (the need to keep interview conditions the same), survey research can generate situated knowledge, that is knowledge inscribed by and not separate from its social location and context, even though the complex nature of this knowledge can be observed in quantitative analysis. The validity so craved may be questioned.

Conclusions

There are some methodological difficulties a race researcher is likely to encounter when using surveys as a tool and these include: problem definition (deciding what kind of answers are required); sample selection (deciding who/what is to be counted); design/ selection of measurements (deciding what is to be measured and how); and questions of social and ethical responsibility (prevention of harm and discomfort).

Holstein and Gubrium (1998; Gubrium and Holstein 2002) argue that in survey research, the research subject is assumed to be 'epistemologically passive' and is seen as a 'vessle-of-answers'. Under 'ideal' conditions, Holstein and Gubrium suggest that survey researchers should be able to give interviewers 'authentic' reports about their feelings, opinions and behaviours. Holloway and Jefferson (2000: 11) have further argued that 'all survey-type research makes certain assumptions about a research participant'. They characterize some of these assumptions as being based upon a research subject who (these are common dilemmas):

- Is knowledgeable about his or her experience (with regard to actions, feelings and perspectives).
- Can access the relevant knowledge accurately and comprehensively (i.e., they have a reliable and accurate memory).
- Can convey the knowledge to a stranger.
- Is motivated to tell the truth.

In all of the elements above the racialized participant is problematic.

Punch (2003) notes the important aspects of survey research are planning, designing, execution, reporting and interpretation of survey research. As De Vaus (2002) argues, you should become a critical consumer of research. He argues that the logic of surveys and statistics is employing an extension of the logic we use in everyday life; analysis, how- ever, requires creativity and imagination rather than the application of sterile mechanical procedures.

Billig et al. (1988) argue that the dilemmas are cultural products, which have a history based in the tensions and the contradictions of modern ideologies. The dilemmas around race research in surveys reflect the utilization and theorization of both the sur- veying technique and the racialized communities. The literature on surveying race does more than just describe the methodological 'problems' and concerns with regard to researching 'race' and ethnicity. The literature – as an example of research as a discursive practice – is also produced by and produces racialized and ethnicized social relations. The process of research, being actively involved in the production of the social meanings of 'race' and ethnicity, takes place at two main levels: (1) through the racialized (gendered and classed) occupational structures of social science institutions that structure the micro interactions of research encounters; and (2) through the epistemological assumptions that are made, and then acted upon, about the nature of racialized subjectivity, inter-subjectivity and difference. These issues are explored in more depth in the following chapter.

The strategy for race researchers should be not to abandon surveys but tackle some of the difficulties by using the tool of reflexivity. This engagement needs to be placed in the wider debate around methodology in sociology (see for example *Sociology* Special Issue 2007). Savage and Burrows (2007), for example, both reject the survey method. They argue that as with interviews, it is a method that is being eclipsed by social transactional research technologies (e.g., geodemographic systems such as Mosaic, see Burrows and Gane 2006). Crompton (2008) advocates caution because while survey research has its limitations and failing response rates are a problem, the capacity of survey research to simultaneously explore the impact of a number of different variables on a particular phenomenon, as well as the relationship between different variables, should not be underestimated. To establish 'enduring regularities' (Savage and Burrows 2007: 889) is not the sole object of survey research. In a similar vein, the indepth interview does not simply give the respondents' 'point of view' but can also, for example, illuminate the 'structural causes that have contributed to particular life choices and outcomes' (Bour-dieu et al. 1999: 623). Savage and Burrows' (2007) advice on abandoning causality and embracing description and classification reflects an assumption that the survey cannot respond to a changing methodological terrain. Crompton and Lyonette (2007), among others, have argued that the surveying technique should be seen as part of the future for social scientists – concerned with a whole array of issues, including race – and not abandoned.

Further reading

Aldridge, A. and Levine, K. (2001) *Surveying the Social World: Principles and Practice in Social Research*. Maidenhead: Open University Press. A practical text giving useful advice to those with limited resources.

Aspinall, P. (2000) Should a question on 'religion' be asked in the 2001 British Census? A public policy case in favour, *Social Policy Administration*, 34(5): 584–600.

Aspinall, P. (2001) Operationalising the collection of ethnicity data in studies of sociology of health and illness, *Sociology of Health and Illness*, 23(6): 828–62.

Czaja, R. and Blair, J. (2004) *Designing Surveys: A Guide to Decisions and Procedures*, 2nd edn. Thousand Oaks, CA: Pine Forge. A comprehensive coverage of the issues involved in surveying. It contains all you need to design and run a professional standard survey.

De Vaus, D. (2002) *Surveys in Social Research*. London: Routledge. This volume provides a good overview of surveys in social science including online resources and all aspects of survey design.

Fowler, F. J. (2002) *Survey Research Methods*, 3rd edn. London: Sage.

Lavrakas, P. J. (1993) *Telephone Survey Methods: Sampling, Selection and Supervision*. London: Sage. This work provides detailed coverage of telephone surveys.

Marsh, C. (1982) *The Survey Method: The Constribution of Surveys to Sociological Explanation*. London: George Allen & Unwin. This provides a good discussion of the criticisms levied at the survey technique.

Punch, K. F. (2003) *Survey Research: The Basics*. London: Sage. A concise, comprehensive 'how to' guide to all aspects of survey research.

Rhodes, P. (1994) Race of interviewer effects in qualitative research: a brief comment, *Sociology*, 28(2): 547–58.

Sapsford, R. (1999) *Survey Research*. London: Sage.

Notes

1   While major large scale studies such as government surveys are discussed, the main emphasis is on small scale projects such as can be carried out by one researcher or a small group.

2   There could be change in which racial groups are externally categorized or categorize themselves, e.g. census case study. An important caveat is that American sociology is dominated by survey analysis (Halsey 2004). Indepth interview preference is something particular to Britain. The minority of qualitative researchers in the US conduct ethnographies or observation studies. Some influential commentators (Goldthorpe 2000; Halsey 2004) see sample surveys as the core methodological resource for sociology.

3   There are many different types of surveys. This book focuses on small scale quantitative surveys because it's aimed at students. The essence of quantitative research is the relationship between variables.

4 Race interviewing

For many researchers, given the problematic nature of quantitative methods as discussed through the example of surveys in the previous chapter, the most productive way of researching race is through the use of qualitative methods (Stanfield and Dennis 1993; Twine and Warren 2000; Gunaratnam 2003; Bulmer and Solomos 2004). Chief among the qualitative methods that have been used to research race, and the focus of this chapter, is indepth interviewing (Payne 2007).[1]

This chapter focuses on the difficulties that researching race is thought to present for indepth interviewing. Particularly on the problem that racial difference between the interviewer and interviewee creates barriers to greater disclosure. Then it will look at the strategies researchers have offered for this perceived difficulty. The first asserts that there should be a match between the race of the interviewer and of the interviewee to ensure that the researcher benefits from an insider position. The second centres on the argument that race in the interview process needs to be more fluidly understood. It cannot be given priority or essentialized and hence cannot be 'matched for'. Refuting the dichotomy of an insider/outsider position, this strategy argues that the interview process needs to be worked towards regardless of the subject matter.

Indepth interview

Indepth, face to face interviewing has become one of the most popular methods of qualitative research.[2] Qualitative interviews, with their focus upon eliciting meaning are different to surveys. While standardization may be the goal of quantitative surveying, in qualitative research the exploration often centres around exploring difference. As Cotterill (1992: 601) has observed 'no two interviews are the same'. Silverman (2001) in *Interpreting Qualitative Data* argues that for some unstructured, open ended interviewing can and does elicit 'authentic accounts of subjective experience'. Qualitative interviews allow researchers to gain a better understanding of the researched life.

There are various conceptions of interviewing and alternate images of the subject behind the interview participant (see Gubrium and Holstein 2002). The two conceptions this chapter will focus on are the interview as an extraction of information and the interview as an interactive process. Recently, the common view of the interview as a one-way pipeline for transporting knowledge has been challenged by the recognition of the interview as a meaning-making conversation – a site and occasion for making meaning. It is more like a two-way informational street than a one-way data pipeline. Furthermore, because it is a two-way conversation, interviewing is always unavoidably interactional and constructive – in brief, the interview is active. From this perspective, it is better to see respondents as participants. They are involved in meaning construction, not contamination. This has heightened the importance of the interaction between the researcher and the researched.

As with many of the research methods discussed in this book, the impact that race is perceived to have will depend on how the method is regarded and how race is understood. In short, many researchers may embark on indepth interviewing but they will each see the point of it very differently. It may serve different researchers in different ways.

The end point of everyone involved is how to get as much out of indepth interviewing as possible, but because they will see the nature of race, the tool of indepth interviewing and the subject differently, they will also differ on how to tackle it.

A particular concern in this chapter is to examine the epistemological assumptions upon which race of interviewer effects have been conceptualized, and how these assumptions relate to notions of racialized inter/subjectivity and 'truth'.

Race difference as a barrier

A large amount of literature has grown around the notion that a difference of race between the interviewer and interviewee creates a barrier to achieving an insider status and maximizing the research potential of indepth interviewing. A key solution to be sought here is how one stops racial difference becoming a barrier.

As Young notes (2004: 187) 'at stake in this debate is an understanding of the extent to which being socially distant or dissimilar to the kinds of people under study affects both the richness or accuracy of the data being collected and the subsequent analysis that unfolds'. A widely held assumption in this debate is that researchers sharing the same social categories memberships as their respondents (for example race, gender and class) were best suited to uncover ideas, arguments and opinions about issues and concerns related to people in these social categories (Merton 1988).

> A corollary presumption was that those researchers who [did] not share such membership either had to work especially hard to acquire the trust and confidence of respondents, or else accept that their scholarly analysis and interpretation may not reflect the veracity, depth, or subtlety that emerges from so-called 'insider' researcher.
>
> (Young 2004: 187)

In reacting to these presumptions, qualitative field researchers strove to address whether and, if so, how greater ease, comfort, comprehension, and transparency could be established in the course of research, especially if such researchers occupied extreme outsider statuses. These efforts led field researchers to explore more critically the epistemological implications of either working to further their insider statuses or to confront the problems resulting from their outsider statuses (Wilson 1974; Baca Zinn 1979; Andersen 1993; DeVault 1995; Naples 1996; Ladner [1973] 1998; De Andrade 2000; Venkatesh 2002).

Young (2004: 188) further notes

> as most of the these discussions centered on exploring the possibilities for increasing, maintaining, or reconciling the difficulties of securing insider status, an implicit value was placed upon the insider position as the location that is

most conducive for data collection. The belief was that functioning from this position would enable the researcher to acquire the most meaningful, accurate, and honest data. Outsider positions were taken to be less constructive, if not all together detrimental, for conducting qualitative research

The nature of interviewing for many relies heavily on the relationship between the interviewer and the respondent. Thus the race of the interviewer will affect research, especially if conducted on race. Race here is something that needs to be shared to be understood and if it is not shared it will not be openly talked about. It may affect the recruitment, participation rate, honesty and level of rapport established. The general consensus seems to be that the greater the commonality between researcher and researched the greater the level of disclosure. This is evidenced by the experience of a number of white researchers researching race who have expressed a number of difficulties of doing research on communities whose racial composition differs from their own.

Case study: 'Race-of-interviewer-effect' in survey research

Riessman (1987) and Reed (2000), among others, have convincingly argued that interviewing without due regard to social, cultural and linguistic differences in the interview can lead to significant misunderstandings and/or misrepresentation that can feed into racist practices and the production of knowledge.

Edwards (1990) has drawn attention to how the race of the interviewer affects access, trust, rapport and talk about private matters in interracial interviewing in feminist research, drawing on her experience as a white middle class woman interviewing African Carribean, mainly working class, women returning to full time education as undergraduates: 'Black women do not talk about all areas of their lives to white women, female researchers in the same easy way that white women do, as a result of their structural position and allegiances in society' (Edwards 1990: 486).

Pause for reflection

List the objectives of indepth interviewing. In what way is racial commonality a way of achieving these and in what way will it hinder you? Would you experience any of the above?

Studies claim that research participants are less willing to tell interviewers from another racial group what they really think regarding their attitudes and opinions about racial topics. Rhodes (1994) notes that the race of interviewer will be a factor particularly in relation to race topics. The race-of-interviewer-effects (RIE) is a term that has been used to refer to the 'response bias and measurement error' that has been recorded in the 'adjustment' that people make to their opinions and attitudes when questioned by an interviewer from another racial or ethnic group.

As Gunaratnam (2003: 54) argues there has been no comparative research in Britain into 'race of interviewer effects' on the scale of US research, however practices of ethnic matching in surveys in Britain have a long history and continue to be used (for example Daniel 1969). This needs to be situated in the wider problematization of interracial research that continues to characterize contemporary research. In interracial interviews research encounter is characterized by distance and estrangement between the researcher and the research participant, which the researcher needs to 'overcome' (Shields 1996; Marcus 1998).

Ethnic matching strategies

Racial matching between interviewers and interviewees has been put forward as a solution to the problems of racialized difference and distance.

Papadopoulos and Lees (2002) in an article on 'culturally competent' research have advocated racial matching between researchers and research participants as an example of 'ethnic sensitivity' in research. They suggest that racial matching should be practiced 'whenever possible', because it:

> encourages a more equal context for interviewing which allows more sensitive and accurate information to be collected. A researcher with the same ethnic background as the participant will possess 'a rich fore understanding' (Ashworth 1986) and an insider/emic view (Leininger 1991; Kauffman 1994), will have more favourable access conditions and the co-operation of a large number of people (Hanson 1994) and a genuine interest in the health and welfare of their community (Hillier and Rachman 1996).
>
> (Papadopoulos and Lees 2002: 261)

Racial matching is a solution not just to cultural and linguistic difference in research interaction – but also it is promoted as reducing intersubjective distances between the interviewer and the research participant (see also Bhopal 2001; Dunbar et al. 2002). An interviewer of the same race enjoys an insider status that someone of a different race does not. Sharing the same race creates an insider status because of the shared cultural attributes, shared language and greater awareness of etiquette and sensitive topics. This will affect the relationship between the interviewer and interviewee, creating trust, rapport and greater edge in what to ask and how, more chance of (continued) participation and good will. This relationship offers a greater chance to be honest and open about a topic as sensitive as race.

Bulmer and Solomos (2004: 2) note that among the 'trends that are discernable in the academic study of race and ethnicity in Western Europe and North America [is] a more racially and ethnically diverse group of scholars has become involved in the field, in marked contrast to the situation a generation ago'. So there are enough researchers to make ethnic matching possible. Many of these have a strong personal and political engagement and location that challenges and questions the traditional white/Other dynamic of much research (Twine 2000).

Pause for reflection

Are you as a researcher limited by your race in terms of what and who you can research?

Duneier (2004: 92) found from his experience of researching race among street vendors in America that though there were differences between him and the vendors along the lines of social class, religion, levels of education and occupation none of these differences seemed to be as significant as that of race. He writes,

> When I stood at Hakim's table, I felt that, as a white male, I stood out. In my mind, I had no place at his table, because he was selling so-called black books. I thought that his product formed the boundary of a sort of exclusionary black zone where African Americans were welcome but whites were not ... Participant observers like myself who do cross race field must, I think, be aware that there are many things members of the different races will not say in one another's presence.
>
> Duneier (2004: 99)

Pause for reflection: On Duneier's experience

In what ways can you see the researcher's assumption of race influencing his approach to the research field? Particularly how does his discomfort with his own racialized position influence his perception of others?

Interviewing rapport is based on more than just race

However, for many the problem and solution identified by the racial matching strategy does not allow a full appreciation of the nature of researching race or the indepth interview. The problem with focusing on achieving greater discloser in indepth interviewing through race matching is in giving priority to race considerations in indepth interviewing that it may not merit.

Misunderstanding race

Racial matching is not really a solution to race interviewing as it leads to a misunderstanding of the nature of race in the interview process. As Gunaratnam (2003: 82) argues, it subsumes the complexities of subjectivity and social positioning under the overarching category of race (or ethnic, cultural, religious and/or linguistic issues). It fails to 'recognize and work through the complexities and contingency of multiple and cross-cutting subjective, biographical and social differences'.

Within matching strategies 'race and/or ethnicity are thus approached (and used) as forms of "methodological capital"' (Gallagher 2000) that can be exploited to build rapport, cooperation and trust, and to gain access to the 'authentic' views and experiences of minoritized research participants. But a deeper exploration uncovers other dynamics submerged in these epistemological assumptions about the nature of racialized inter/subjectivity in the interview. Race and ethnicity in research with minoritized research participants from the perspective of racial matching strategies are seen as defining the emotional and ethnical dimensions of the interview interaction in ways that eclipse differences in gender, class, age, disability and sexuality.

Matching for one social identity fails to take into account the dynamic interplay of social differences and identifications. For example, the reality is that race is always classed and gendered. In short, racial matching is not sufficient and it does not provide a solution to creating the condition for greater disclosure in the interview process. This solution also works with a particular view of the interview and the respondent.

Case study

Song and Parker (1995), when recounting their experiences of indepth interviewing with Chinese and British born Chinese people as Korean American and British born Chinese researchers, respectively, point to the problems of a black/white binary and the cul-de-sac invoked through colour based ascription: 'racialised categories applied to the researcher and the researcher are conceptualized as too rigid and homogenous. "Black" juxtaposed to "white", does not easily accommodate individuals who are of mixed descent, or who are bi-cultural [sic], and suggest too unitary an experience of ethnic minority status' (1995: 242–3). Their experience and one that race researchers should adopt is to appreciate that they should not assume a racial category. Song and Parker recollect how they were frequently involved in a process of 'circling' with respondents in which, as researchers, they are 'sized up' and located dichotomously as either British or Chinese, a process that in actuality is fraught with multiple misrecognition. These multiple positionings of researchers serve to rewrite the rubric which construes race subjectivities to be fixed and unchanging. In a similar post-race vein Rhodes, through a methodological consideration of the subject, reflects how 'The significance of skin colour was rarely the same from start to finish of an interview and more was gained from considering it as an interactive factor in the dynamic context of each interview than from attempting to isolate it as a variable' (1994: 552). This is also Nayak's (2006) experience of conducting ethnography where he has been positioned as Asian, Black, British, Indian, Scouse and, rather less ceremoniously, 'that Paki'. Others have written about similar experiences (see Ramji 2007).

This is usefully linked to the post-race approach discussed earlier in this volume. Instead of seeing race as a dimension we bring to the interviewing table, a post-race reading would stress the *impossibility* of this identity. There is no racial subject that prefigures interaction. It is something 'we do rather than are' (Nayak 2006: 426). Your race is not simply read off your ontological body. The radical potential of post-race perspective, Nayak (2006: 426) argues, lies in the understanding that our identities are produced in the interview encounter itself rather than coming to precede the event.

His (2006: 96) first rule in researching race through indepth interviewing is 'don't begin with the assumption that special rapport or trust is always a precondition for doing successful fieldwork. And don't be so presumptuous as to believe that you have trust or even special rapport with the people you are trying to write about, even when it seems you do'.

In the approach advocated by the matching strategy, race is being reified. By racial matching you are assuming the race of the respondent.

Exploring the 'insider/outsider' boundary

It is useful to explore this with regard to the experiences of how researchers/interviewers from groups racialized as 'ethnic minorities' have accounted for our own complex social and political locations, and the production and effects of these in interview encounters.

Pause for reflection

If you are thinking of researching a community that you consider yourself to be from, what is likely to be your main concern:

1 Do you think you will have some unique insight?
2 What sort of pressure are you likely to feel from those you are researching?
3 Do you think you face unique ethical dilemmas?

Alexander's work on black (1996) and Asian (2000) youth demonstrates the ambiguous position of 'native' ethnographers. In what ways did her insider/outsider status become manifest and help/hinder her research?

Case study: Native researcher ambiguity

Claire Alexander (2004: 136) draws on her ethnographies of black and Asian youth, *The Art of Being Black* (1996) and *The Asian Gang* (2000), to reflect on the position of 'native' ethnographers. She writes,

> I was too 'native' to be professional, too close to be objective, and altogether too Asian. More generally, it marks me alternatively as gatekeeper, apologist or traitor.
>
> While I would acknowledge that my identification as 'Asian' facilitated my access initially, it was neither a sufficient nor simple foundation for the relationships that emerged later. Nor were these relationships based on ideas of shared 'culture', but on a less tangible set of alliances and hard won mutual trust and affection.
>
> (2004: 145)

She allowed them to choose their names, in returning their 'voices' on the tapes at the end of the project, in the writing up, through their involvement in the reading and editing process.

As a minority researcher you will find a surprisingly small literature that explores and theorizes the specific experiences of interviewers from minority groups. There is an implicit assumption that there won't be any difficulties.

There is little theoretical and methodological knowledge to draw upon to guide the development of interviewing practices. Critiquing 'standpoint epistemology' Brah (1996: 207) has suggested that minoritized 'positionality' can create specific opportunities for the understanding of difference but 'it does not in itself assure a vantage point of privileged insight into and understanding of relations of power'. She challenges the inherent race consciousness of both minoritized research participants and interviewers. Phoenix similarly insists that 'different types of accounts about "race" and racism are produced by black and white interviewers of both colours [sic] whenever possible since it illustrates that ways in which knowledges are "situated"' (1996: 66).

Young (2004) among others advocates a re-assessment of the 'outsider' status in qualitative research in general and indepth interviewing in particular. The search for increased insider status is narrow and misses the fact that rapport can be lost by the occupation of certain insider statuses.

We might be viewed as an insider by a community for whom we think we are an outsider, or as outsiders in a community we thought we were part of. Song and Parker (1996) and Ramji (2008) all speak of the difficulty of commonality and difference in the research process. De Andrade (2000) has written about the difficulty of respondents being unable to immediately discern whether the researcher occupied an ethnic insider status relevant to the research agenda. In analysing her experiences she argued that the insider position is not fixed or static, it is instead dynamic. It is continually recreated throughout the course of one's fieldwork. Her interviews, then, were serial experiences in working to establish, and continually maintain, an insider status throughout the conversations.

Reinharz (1997) similarly asserts that one or more of a researcher's multiple selves may become relevant in the interactive dynamics of fieldwork. These multiple selves include a researcher's race, gender or class status, as well as varied aspects of their personality or personal experiences. If they do not appear at first sight, any of them could become visible to respondents and informants during the course of fieldwork. More importantly, respondents and informants may react to any of these in ways that foster, hinder or dramatically affect conversations with the research. In essence, respondents and informants may react to any of these in ways that foster, hinder or dramatically affect conversations with the researcher. In essence, respondents and informants may use these features and characteristics to determine the ways in which that researcher is an outsider or insider, and to adjust their interaction with the researcher accordingly throughout an interview or fieldwork encounter.

Young notes (2004: 191)

> these and other investigations have led to the contemporary assertion that there is no singular insider or outsider position that researchers occupy during the course of fieldwork, but rather myriad positions and statues that can be viewed by respondents either as insider or outsider depending on the social circumstances or conditions affecting the research endeavor (De Andrade 2000; Jackson 2001; Naples 1996; Reinharz 1997). Accordingly, the distinction between insider and outsider status should best be thought of as an analytical rather than

experiential divide. Moreover, it has now been accepted that insider and outsider positions are fluid as they are continually restructured, retained and abandoned during the course of interaction between researchers and respondents (De Andrade 2000; Naples 1996; Reinharz 1997; Riessman 1987; Song and Parker 1995). These more recent commentators have demonstrated that insider status, though crucial for the ultimate advance of field research, is neither easily attainable nor consistently maintainable. Thus, although researchers continue to strive to maximize their insider status, in fact they stand experientially in the midst of ever-shifting configurations of both positions.

Despite the recent advances, an enduring value is still placed upon the insider status as being the privileged position from which to converse with respondents. This means that researchers ultimately aim to increase their insiderness even if they know that they must contend with the various issues concerning outsiderness. Consequently there is a lack of more critical exploration of how insider status may, in fact, inhibit conversation during specific moments in fieldwork.

Case study

Twine, an African American researcher makes an important point about the differential identifications among 'racial subalterns' which problematize neat insider and outsider dichotomies. Drawing upon her research in Brazil, Twine has written about the entangled relations between subjectivity, identification and social location, such that the Brazilians of African descent that she interviewed frequently did not express a different political standpoint on issues of racism to white people. Moreover, in relation to interviewing, Twine contends that:

> rather than mistrusting a white researcher, racial subalterns in Brazil may be more likely to identify with them. My experiences suggest that some Brazilians of color do not necessarily feel comfortable discussing the topic of race and racism with those who resemble them racially ... Moreover, prestige hierarchies and the valorization of whiteness resulted in some Brazilians of color preferring to be interviewed by my white partner.
>
> (Twine 2000: 16)

Futhermore, it could be argued that the biases and shortcomings associated with a researcher's occupation of an outsider status can sometimes be overcome or managed by the researcher's explicit acknowledgement of the existence of social distance or categorical dissimilarities between him or her and the individuals under study (Waters 1999; Venkatesh 2000; Lamont 2002; Bourgois 2003).

Outsider status in certain cases can stimulate important and revealing conversations in the field. Young (2004) makes his case by assessing his experiences in a long-standing engagement in what immediately appears to be straightforward insider situated research, as an African American man researching African American males of the same age and socio-economic background regarding their perceptions of social mobility.

From basic categorical standpoint, I appear to have been an extreme insider in the course of this work. However, the truth of the matter is that at certain moments this experience has been riddled with moments of bewilderment, confusion, and tension, all of which resulted from assumptions that some of these men made about me on the basis of assumed insider connections. In the course of my fieldwork and in the years that followed, I have been drawn to think about the sometimes crippling effects of insider status [i.e. the rupturing of rapport with those individuals whom I studied] and the benefits that may come from being a compassionate outsider...

Rapport is immediately assumed to be a product of interaction predicted upon two principal features associated with insider status: intimacy and trustworthiness. The comfort or familiarity that comes with insider status can also promote impatience or confusion when one or more of the interacting parties does not seem to follow, the implicit rules of dialogue for people who are familiar with each other. Put more specifically, one may feel that he or she should not have to say certain things to familiar others because those others should already be 'in the know'. Being asked to say something about those things can rupture or at least disturb rapport. A number of encounters that I experienced in my fieldwork demonstrated this fact.

(Young 2004: 194)

Young (2004: 197) felt that if he was an outsider, even with all the problems these would have included, it is quite possible that men in his studies might have been prepared to explain more fully or further elucidate their views resulting in the emergence of a broader and more expansive narrative. Thus, a different, and in some ways potentially more comprehensive, insight into how these men take stock of themselves as social actors might have been produced from their having to speak to people who they construed as outsiders to their experiences and social environments. Instead, in these cases his insider status averted rather than extended the conversation.

Case study

Miller's study involved indepth, open-ended interviews with young female mainly black African American gang members. These followed completion of a survey interview by the same researcher. The survey gathered information on a wide range of topics, including the individual, his or her school, friends, family, neighbourhood, delinquent involvement arrest history and victimization, in addition to information about the gang. The indepth interviews were concerned exclusively with the roles and activities of young women in youth gangs, and the meanings they describe as emerging from their gang affiliation. Miller's status differed from her respondents because she was older, white and middle class. Miller's interviews, unlike those conducted by her African American male researcher, often elicited more and different types of detail. Her outsider status was seen as beneficial once trust had been established. The respondents explained things in greater detail because they did not assume any prior knowledge. Her African American researcher similarly thought he intuitively knew what was meant by terms and did not ask for greater elaboration. Social distances in this instance facilitated respondents' recognition of themselves as experts on their social worlds. A level of trust was most important here. Social distances that include differences in relative power can result in suspicion and lack of trust, both of which the researcher must actively seek to overcome. Rapport building is key to this process. Establishing trust and familiarity, showing genuine interest, assuring confidentiality and not being judgemental are important elements of rapport building. Miller's research design proved useful in alleviating tensions that could result from her outsider status. She began with the administration of a survey interview, which began with relatively innocuous questions (demographics) to more sensitive ones about gang involvement. With the survey she established a relationship with each young woman. She also assured them of confidentiality, for example if names were mentioned she erased them on tape in front of the interviewees.

Frankenberg rather controversially has suggested 'that there is a cultural/racial specificity to white people, at times more obvious to people who are not white than to white individuals' (1993: 5). It is certainly the case that many ethnic minorities have historically had to become skilled interpreters of whiteness (hooks 1992; Nayak 1997; Nebeker 1998), but it still must be queried whether there is really a 'racial specificity' to white people, and if so what it looks like (Nayak 2006: 417). However, her point does allow an understanding of how outsider status in researching whiteness can be an advantage.

It is useful to reflect on Reinharz's notion of multiple selves mentioned earlier as a strategy here. Young (2004: 198–9) writes 'While researchers cannot be in full control of how they are located by the people who they study, they can think about the fieldwork experience as involving an amalgamation of insider and outsider positionings that come together to open up as well as resist access to data. The challenge, then, is for researchers to strive to maintain a critical reflexivity about this as they work to negotiate the ever-shifting terrain of relating to respondents in field research'.

Two researchers have recently highlighted the benefits of outsider status. Patricia Hill Collins (1993) discusses what she calls the 'outsider-within' and 'insider-without' circumstances affecting the lives of upwardly mobile African American women; Venkatesh (2002) is another good example.

These debates occupy a significant epistemological and methodological space in empirical research concerned with 'race', and as such are a key site for the production of racialized discourses and practices. In assuming that race will affect the interview encounter we are in some ways reifying race in this way. It may be a good idea to see indepth interviewing as a way of discovering how race is created. Thus the interviewer's position is a tool itself to discover how race is made–unmade.

Reflexivity would enable researchers to scrutinize their own ideological frameworks, research tools and practices. Gill (1998), however, has highlighted the limits of reflexivity because some aspects of ourselves may be beyond self-conception. Researching a racially different group may actually be good for the researcher's development. Lamont (2004: 168) for example notes that before interviewing North African immigrants living in Paris, despite living in the city for four years, she actually had very little contact with this population. 'Discovering their lives, their world views, their families, and their houses was a challenging and a powerful experience for me and, often, for them. A great many of them had had very little experience interacting with European women before our encounter. Indeed, one of them even confessed that our exchange was the first opportunity of this sort he had ever had, although he had been living in France for more than 20 years'.

Another difficulty with the racial matching solution is that it reinforces the idea that race is about non-white groups. While ethnic researchers are employed to work on projects they rarely work without a white research leader. However projects on researching whiteness nearly always involve white interviewers and white research participants (for a critique of this position, see Gallagher 2000). This reproduces whiteness as the undifferentiated norm that is simultaneously naturalized and deproblematized as 'non-racial' (Ware 1992; Frankenberg 1993; Roediger 1994).

Indeed the process of racial matching has specific dilemmas for the race researcher. Some writers have found that they may by reluctant to undertake race research because they don't want to be labeled and thus experience lack of career mobility as a 'minority researcher', they might also be accused of being biased, or accused by their community of 'selling out' to the dominant White culture (Cox and Nkomo 1990).

Case study

Anoop Nayak (2006: 416) argues that Frankenberg's study of the social construction of whiteness (race) is ultimately grounded in the corporeal certainty of her respondents, so called 'white-women'. By conflating whiteness as a social process – fluid, malleable and endlessly reconstituted – with a secure, apparently knowable object, 'white women', we are left with the tangible irreducibility of race'. Inevitably in researching whiteness, Frankenberg is drawn to interviewing and seeking out 30 'white women in particular' (p. 35) and forced to negotiate an uneasy path to access respondents whereupon, 'a call for white women only could sound like blatant discrimination' (p. 34). This creates a subtle, politically significant, but somewhat unresolvable, paradigmatic tension. To what extent is whiteness a social construction if it is always reliant upon a white subject to enact and materialize it? As Gunaratnam has recently noted, 'despite theoretical understandings of "race" and ethnicity as relational and socially constructed, there is still a voracious appetite for approaches that freeze, objectify and tame "race"/ethnicity into unitary categories that can be easily understood and managed' (2003: 33). The problematic of why whiteness as a *practice* is collapsed into the social category 'white people', and its implications for our understanding of race, are worthy of closer scrutiny.

Nayak (2006: 417) further writes that 'Frankenberg begins with a stark declaration "that there *is* a cultural/racial specificity to white people, at times more obvious to people who are not white than white individuals"'. While many ethnic minorities have historically had to become skilled interpreters of whiteness (hooks 1992; Nayak 1997; Nebeker 1998), it is worth asking: is there really a 'racial specificity' to white people, and if so what exactly does it look like? Instead, he suggests that cultures are far more porous and promiscuous than implied and are forever subject to change. Thus is his ethnography of race, class and contemporary youth formations in Britain it seemed difficult to isolate white ethnicity in global times from what remains a thoroughly chequered cultural tapestry of sustained black–white interaction (Nayak 2003). Moreover, whiteness is not homogenous but fractured by the myriad ethnic practices of Russian Jews, Poles, Italians or Irish people (to say nothing of the individual ways they may 'live' ethnicity). He suggests that the seemingly knowable object Frankenberg identifies, 'white woman', cannot be understood outside of the specific historical and geographical processes that constitute this subjectivity as intelligible, and the symbolic regimes of language that summon this representation to life. This is reflective of Said's (1978) and Fanon's (1986) idea that races reflect one another and operate in binaries. For Fanon there is no recourse to blackness or whiteness as 'proper objects', but rather as an ontological critique of the arbitrary sign-making system that makes them appear true: 'Ontology – once it is finally admitted as leaving existence by the wayside – does not permit us to understand the being of the black man. For not only must the black man be black; he must be black in relation to the white man' (Fanon [1952] 1970: 77).

The literature of researching 'threatening topics' may also be of use here to develop techniques in asking questions that can either desensitize (Sudman and Bradburn 1974, 1982) or 'de-jeopardize' (Warner 1965; Tracy and Fox 1981) threatening topics. While by no means universally agreed or supported, the rationale behind such techniques is that purposeful changes in the design and administration of interviews can be used to reduce threat and therefore maximize disclosures. Safe and dangerous topics, however, will change in the course of an interview. But an interview could start based upon a norm of safe topics and research interactions in which the research participant is positioned as comfortable, open and disclosing. Within such as scenario, interactional relations, particularly power relations, can escape detailed analytical attention – as we have become focused upon why research participants do not talk about certain subjects, rather than examining why and when they talk about others.

From this it transpires that whiteness or blackness is not attached to respective white and black bodies but rather that race signs are encoded into everyday practice. It reveals also that signifiers of black and white are relational and mutually constitutive.

Case study

Lamont (2002: 162) (Bulmer and Solomos 2004) has a different understanding of race in the interview process. One that accepts that the interviewee will inevitably affect the interview. Lamont's work which resulted in the books *The Dignity of Working Men: Morality and the Boundaries of Race, Class and Immigrant* (Lamont 2000) preceded by *Money, Moral and Manners: The Culture of the French and the American Upper Middle Class* (Lamont 1992) meant interviewing through gender, class, colour, global inequality, religion, different colonial empires and age. While some identities like national and professional identity were 'fungible' (p. 163) others like gender were not.

As a French Canadian, Lamont believed the North African immigrants to France and African Americans opened up more. Moreover she sustained 'this blurring' by maintaining 'a certain vagueness in my responses to their question concerning my own life, adopting a kind of psychoanalytical non-interventionist pose throughout the interviews, and I resisted opening up until after the interview/ experiment had ended, to the extent that it was possible' (p. 165).

In a direct engagement with the RIE literature she argues that the interview is still a useful device that

> is not about oneself. It is about the other, and about presenting oneself as a template against which the other can bounce his/her identity and world view. The interviewee will of course respond to the identity of the inter-viewer, but first and foremost, she or he should be entering into an exchange where she or he becomes intimately engaged with a stranger, even if it is to respond to the stimuli presented by the stranger's identity ... The fact that the participant knows that she or he will never see the stranger again can facilitate this process: it provides reassurance that the interview is not the beginning of a relationship, but a micro-episode unnaturally isolated from everyday life.
>
> (2002: 165)

For Lamont the interviewer should stay the same for all the interviews because then we can see how different populations respond to the same stimuli: 'In this context, it is crucial *not* to match interviews and respondents by race, ethnicity, gender etc.: That different respondents read the stimuli represented by an inter-viewer differently is part of the data on the "us/them" boundary and should not be edited out of the interview situation' (2002: 166). Undoubtedly, an Asian will speak differently about their identity to another Asian than a non Asian. But that is not to deny that both conservations are valuable and reflect their reality.

While cautioning that 'it' does not always work, she argues that 'the art and science of interviewing consists in having the ability to create a delicate balance between setting the agenda for an interview, and bracketing one's identity. The bracketing works only if the participant perceives the interviewer as having a sympathetic ear, even if the interviewee is describing the most horrific racist, ethnocentric, Darwinist representations of the world. When it works, trust, and a great interview, are the outcome (Lamont 2002: 166).

Connectivity as a strategy in indepth interviewing

Gunaratnam (2003) in challenging the assertion that racialized commonalities are critical to the success of interracial interviewing, argues for a move from naturalized commonality to a worked for connectivity, in which the recognition of points of difference, their meanings and effects are vital. The messy, complex and dynamic nature of interracial interviewing should be valued, worked through – and even enjoyed! The researcher should understand the social world, the interview and the individuals in it as all different (Harding 1987; Silverman 2003). These arguments are well rehearsed in the qualitative approach literature (see Silverman 2003) and the 'active interview' (Holstein and Gubrium 1998) which sees both parties in the interview as necessarily and unavoidably active. It is interesting to look at the processes that make up this active interview, as it is not just about having the right question for the right answer.

Normalizing interviewing across race

As Fowler (2002: 122) writes 'In general, a researcher would be best advised to send the best interviewer available to interview a respondent, regardless of demographic characteristics'. Creating empathy with the respondent is a necessary element to them freely participating. Once it is appreciated that race is constructed in the interview process and the researcher is not in a natural position. Then we can argue that a solution of doing a good interview is about being a good interviewer.

Pause for reflection: Ways of dealing with difference in indepth interviews

Interviewer's role – What can you do to create a good interview situation regardless of the topic?

1   Gain cooperation.
2   Train and motivate respondents.
3   Be a standardized interviewer.
4   Present the study.
5   Ask questions and probe.
6   Record the answers.
7   Develop interpersonal relations.

Multiple interviews for Edwards (1990) gave her a chance to establish rapport. She did not see the solution as racial matching. The lessons she learnt from her research were:

1   Access: in doing research in/through institutions, white women researchers need to consider how 'black' women may experience the institution, particularly in terms of racialized, gendered and class related practices, and take these experiences into account when recruiting women into research studies. Assumptions about the status and credulity of institutional associations that can enable access to white research participants cannot be granted. Edwards states: 'When I contacted black women through … educational institutions, I was that institution, defined as white, middle class and oppressive' (1990: 485).
2   Trust: trust can be built through explicit attention to confidentiality and discussion of the researcher's approach to the representation of interview accounts.

3   Rapport: rapport can be facilitated by an acknowledgement of racialized difference in terms of both structural power relations and how it can affect the understanding of interview accounts.
4   Talk about 'private' matters: discussion of 'private' matters such as family relationships can be enabled through multiple interviews with the same participant, when time is taken to build up rapport with the interviewing relationship.

Many researchers including Edwards and Alexander have found making a commitment to respondents at the end of the research to present their analysis and findings of the completed project to them useful. This is reflective of an ethnical responsibility to include respondents but also an epistemological and methodological awareness that they create knowledge and have agency and interaction in the research process which means these must be catered for. It is a well rehearsed argument that in an individual interview, (Wieviorka 2004: 62)

> the researcher seeks to understand and not simply record the facts of the situation and has to create a minimum feeling of empathy with the person questioned quite simply to make them want to participate in the discussion. The researcher knows that he is not in a purely neutral position. He has to respect the person being interviewed, take him or her seriously, push them to do as far as possible in thinking about the themes discussed; now, if this person is racist, this type of position is difficult. The researcher in this case may be tempted to conceal his opinions. He may, for example, elicit racist remarks, present himself as having the same ideas and the same prejudice, and put his interviewee at ease by adopting a racist stance himself.

Wieviorka's (2004: 62) instructions to his team were to be 'researchers the whole time – we are not there either to accept to reject the remarks made, but to understand them and to enable those who make them to think about them'.

Case study: Establishing credibility and rapport. Cultural sensitivity without racial matching

Historically, African Americans have often been the subjects of research studies without their consent, yet few of these studies yielded benefits to this racial group (Jones 1993; Home Office 2001). Some African American communities and community members believe they will continue to be exploited by researchers. Although the Tuskegee experiment serves as a constant reminder of experimentation without consent, there are other examples of other research related atrocities (Gamble 1993; Jones 1993; Dula 1997; Home Office 2001). Even if the research is reasonable, it may be met with significant distrust because of the past relationship between this minority group and the research profession (Gamble 1993). Communities history with research is important when trying to secure responses.

A good way of establishing credulity and rapport, a major step in research and important whether the respondent is white and or part of a minority group, could be achieved by the following. The participants, and others in the community (e.g., community leaders), must be informed of why the research is being done and how the data will be used. Credulity can be enhanced by giving meaningful roles to participants during the research process and by establishing a climate of openness, respect and shared information. The researcher can establish legitimacy by working through traditional gatekeepers in the community, the church, education and business leaders (Vaz 1997). If these gatekeepers accept the legitimacy of the research (and the scholar), they can make the introductions necessary for the researcher to make the contacts for collecting data.

Case study: Conducting research with American Indian communities

There are a number of research strategies that have been recommended in the literature (Mihesuah 1993; McDonald and McAvoy 1997). The researcher will have to gain approval from both the legal tribal authority (tribal council) and from the local cultural committees and authorities (e.g., elders council). The researcher has to be introduced to the community by a community member, in reality a process of having a trusted community member vouch for the integrity of the researcher. The researcher has to be seen as someone who is interested and committed enough to spend the necessary time in the community and in attending events.

Methods used for the study will be best accepted if they reflect the traditional epistemology of American Indians. Traditionally, the transmission of knowledge in these cultures has occurred experientially and orally, usually through a series of stages based on the assessment of readiness. Qualitative and participatory methods in the social sciences best mirror American Indian traditional means of communicating knowledge (Conti 1997). The studies that have achieved successful response rates all used personal, semi-structured interviews (McDonald and McAvoy 1997). Focus groups have also been employed successfully in some studies. They seem to be most effective when respondents are brought together on a specific tangible topic (Dunn and Feather 1998). Mailed surveys have usually not been a successful approach with this population. Zivot (1979) tried this approach in a study of native communities in northern Canada and received a zero response rate.

Analysis of data in studies focused on American Indians should be done with community members, and subsequent results should be reviewed by and shared with the local community. Some communities may require that any publication arising from research in that community be reviewed by a tribal cultural committee for accuracy. The issues of cultural misinterpretation and community harm are real concerns of American Indian communities, grounded more often than not in past experience (Deloria 1991; Wax 1991). The issue is not just of community harm, which is, however, paramount. But the issue is also that of missing the point because of the ethnocentric blinders of the researcher and the epistemological boundaries of Western science. A cooperative approach to data analysis, interpretation and dissemination can help alleviate these problems.

Gunaratnam's (2003: 7) worked for 'connectivity' is a useful approach to adopt in qualitative research. She advocates using poststructuralist critiques of essentialism in research, while also seeking to legitimate the everyday 'situated voices' (Lewis 2000). In very broad terms this approach recognizes the dynamic constitution of the meanings of 'race' through social discourse and through the subjective investments of individuals (see Brah 1996; Hall 1996). Rather than using a model of research that privileges one person's understanding over another she draws upon Bakhtin's (1981) ideas on 'dialogism' to suggest that research should be concerned with the nature of the difference and the dialogue between the research and the research participant (see also Ali 2006; Ramji 2008).

Power and researcher participant inclusion

Approaches that stress the value of difference and the co-construction of meaning in research span a range of theoretical perspectives. However, what these varied approaches have in common is that they serve to problematize long-standing methodological practices and epistemological assumptions in cross-cultural methodological practices and epistemological assumptions in cross-cultural research, bringing questions of power and of ethics to the communication process (Spivak 1992; Schutte 2000). This attention to power relations in research across racialized and ethnicized difference, together with the more general move towards approaches that have questioned the inherently representational nature of language (Hollway and Jefferson 2000; Poland 2002) have had far reaching consequences (Gunaratnam 2003: 138).

Racial matching does not equalize the power discrepancy in the interview process. It is complacent to think that this does not need to be worked for.

Methodological discussions of interracial qualitative interviewing have traditionally been based upon a number of assumptions. By 'assumptions' she means the nature and effects of interracial encounters are prejudged, taken for granted and/or 'known' *before* any research interaction has taken place (for an insightful discussion on the already recognized 'stranger', see Ahmed 2000).

For Shields (1996) the overriding goal of shared meaning, accompanied by interactional 'rapport' and 'intimacy' can obscure forms of difference and power relations within the research encounter.

While one cannot remove the dynamics of power (Ali 2003), awareness of them can help counteract their negative impact on the research. Thus reflexivity is a useful strategy. Anderson, a white American feminist researcher, has argued that for white women doing research with women 'of colour', it is vital that reflexivity by the researcher includes specific attention to the production of white privilege in the research process. Such reflexitivity should be an integral part of analysis:

> Building more inclusive ways of seeing requires scholars to take multiple views of their subjects, abandoning the idea that there is a singular reality that social science can discover ... how, in constructing sociological analyses, can dominant group members examine their own racial identities and challenge the societal systems of racial stratification in which they observe is situated?
>
> (Anderson 1993: 43)

> Self-examination of my own privilege as a white scholar facilitated this research project, allowing me to challenge the arrogance that the stand of white privilege creates.
>
> (1993: 50–1)

The limitations that may be present in indepth interviewing may be reduced by combining them with other qualitative methodology. Combination with other research approaches in the oral tradition. Vaz (1997) argues these have been successful in the black community. These include participant observation, personal interviews, historical reviews and focus groups (Collins and Butcher 1983; Stanfield 1993). Participant observation provides an opportunity for the researcher to hear, see and experience reality as the participants do, by spending time in the setting. A researcher can combine the efforts of participant observation with establishing credibility within the community by volunteering at a local community school, a community association or other relevant organization. Personal interviews can also be an effective approach because they help the researcher establish a rapport with the community and community members. These indepth interviews can allow the researcher to understand more fully motives and values along with behaviour (McCraken 1988; Hertz 1997). For example Vaz (1997) asserts that during this exchange it is the 'side-chats' that take place outside the parameters of the 'official interview questions' that provide the most insight. Consequently, the researcher has to be flexible enough in the research protocol to allow this data to be considered part of the study. In addition, focus groups have been successfully applied with groups of African American college students (Blahna and Black 1993) and with members of an African American church group (Winter 1998).

There are some strategies that work with some communities, conventionally gatekeepers have been used in researching Asian communities. These have been criticized, however, for usually being old, traditional men, and may not necessarily produce a reflective sample (Ramji 2008).

To do this is to accept that race is not the definer of a community and a shared race will not be enough.

Visual methodology

Case study: Combining approaches and reflexivity

Ali (2006) attempted to use ethnographic practices along with indepth interviewing to try and engage her research subjects in the process, to 'give voice' and authority to groups usually considered 'unreliable' respondents, to make them visible (including literally) through the use of narrative and photography, and to position herself reflexively in this encounter. The reality was more problematic – focusing particularly on the use of visual material, Ali explores the contradictory ways in which the material was produced and interpreted, and the conflict that took place in the struggle for the authorial voice. Ali reflects that, with the benefit of hindsight, her work was only partially successful in alleviating the workings of power inherent in ethnographic research, and that she had underplayed the ways in which both researcher and researched are placed within broader structural processes of power and 'subjection'. She argues that 'reflexivity' is crucial in recognizing and resisting subjection, although it only partially mediates research relationships and often constitutes an 'illusion of agency' rather than anything more substantial.

Ali's (2006: 471) work takes as its starting point the importance of under-standing processes of racialization and draws upon ethnographic work with chil-dren in order to explore the role of reflexivity in managing issues of power in knowledge production. Using the concept of 'subjectivation' it argues that we cannot ever hope to escape (non-)hierarchal power relations in research, that all research is inevitably, to an extent, racializing. Researchers need to understand that there is an integral relationship between knowledge and power. In her case it was important to consider that while education ethnographies might utilize creative approaches to writing, they must attend to the fact that work in educational sites should/might have policy implications. What will schools or colleges be able to do with your ethnography? She worked with children aged 8–11 in three schools, two in London, one in a semi-rural southern town, for a period of 18 months (Ali 2006: 477). She developed a number of interlocking epistemological and methodological strategies. Her decision to use ethnography involved the following concerns: (1) not to rely on any one isolated method such as qualitative indepth interviews; (2) to centralize her own positionality in the research; (3) to utilize the concept of 'reflexivity' as a form of 'managing' power relations. She employed multiple methods including: interviewing, focus groups, observation, textual and archival analysis. She specifically engaged with her own interest in the limits to the lan-guage of 'race' for exploring meanings of mixedness by drawing upon a range of visual methodologies. Given that commonsense ideas of 'race' are often reliant upon 'visual clues', it seemed an obvious choice to use visual materials to explore children's understandings of 'race'. A great deal has been said about the way in which visual methods can complement, or even better, other methods that rely on spoken language or on observations. All the children took part in the initial group discussions which incorporated some use of visual materials from popular culture and which she videotaped. As children began to talk about their identities she began to interview in pairs or alone those who claimed some kind of 'mixed' identity. At this stage she moved on to using family photographs. Rather than starting with pictures that already existed, she gave children disposable cameras, a technique that has since become commonplace, so that they could make their own collection. She did this in order to try and give the children a stake in the research process and allow them to have some control over the production of the data. Their brief was to take pictures of things that meant 'home' and 'family'. She hoped that she would get to see a range of cultural artefacts and practices in situ, and that she would see people who were important to children's understandings of sameness and difference in interethnic families. Once photographs had been processed, the children came and discussed the images with her. They talked her through the images and she asked questions about content and meaning. She intended this process to allow children to analyse their own data and so lead to a better understanding of the role of family life and home in relation to the central pro-blematic of 'racialization' (also see Twine 2006). The results of course are not quite what she expected. Many images did not fulfil the brief, some families didn't want to take part, etc. There were times when she had a completely different reading of what was going on in the images than the children did, reflecting what Bhatt (2004) has called a 'narcissistic streak' in interpreting work on identity and difference.

Pink (2001), among others, notes how reflexivity is an important part of visual research methodologies including video. She engages with some of the critical debates in this area, which is useful to reflect upon before selecting this method. Holliday's (2000: 517) sees her video diary approach as a 'new form of research'. Pink (2001) argues that the 'video diary' approach is innovative in some ways, however the practice of giving cameras to native collaborators in research has formed an important part of the last 25 years of visual anthropology. The potential for empowerment and self-representation for racially marginalized community has been seen as immense. Eric Michaels, for example, developed an innovative project with Australian aboriginals, facilitating their use of video media to represent themselves. In the 1980s Michaels was contracted to 'assess the impact of television on remote Aboriginal communities' (Ruby 2000: 225). To do this he developed a project designed to not only 'study' the aboriginals, but also to give them agency. Rather than simply carrying out an ethnography of their television viewing he trained them in video production and facilitated their setting up of a low power transmission facility so that they could respond to television through their own broadcasts (Ruby 2000: 227). Michaels' work showed how the Aboriginals' approach to the ownership, inheritance and use of information is different from 'European cultures'. The video method not only allowed him to understand dif-ferences between Aboriginal and European use of visual representation and infor-mation but also it empowered his respondents in a global media context in which they might be seen as marginal or 'invisible'.

Two recent writers have explored the growing engagement with the visual in eth-nographic research, specifically the role of photography and how it can be used alongside indepth interviewing to research race. Both Twine (2006) and Knowles (2006) engage critically with the role of the visual in ethnography – challenging the status of the visual as 'real', or as 'speaking for itself' (Banks 2001; Pink 2001). In very different settings, and using very different materials, these articles explore what the visual can add as a meth-odological device – a way of getting research respondents to reflect on their lives and as a form of data – making visible what might otherwise go unmarked and unchallenged. Both authors insist, however, that the visual can only be understood within, and against, ethnographic narrative – it tells a story that may reflect or subvert what is spoken, that may add to the story or tell a different one. The conjunction or disjunction of picture and story can prove at once a productive and disruptive element in ethnographic work. In this way, perhaps, the visual works in a way analogous to the ethnographer's gaze as requiring both interpretative validation and autonomy (Alexander 2006: 405).

Twine (2006) explores the use of family photos in her research on interracial families in Leicester. Family photos, she argues, are not produced as primary ethnographic data (in contrast, for example, to the photos used by Ali 2003), but can be used to 'map' interracial intimacies and to elicit narratives about key moments or transformations in an individual's or group's racial history.

Knowles (2003) uses photos taken by a professional photographer, Douglas Harper, as part of her study of whiteness in Hong Kong. Photographs can, she argues, be an important device in making whiteness visible in its most quotidian performance. In the postcolonial space this provides an important way of researching race, which compliments indepth interview follow-ups. These images must be read in combination with narrative text 'to disrupt, to support or reconfigure existing ways of thinking about and seeing the world'.

Pause for reflection

In what ways are photos problematic? How important is it to know who took them and in what context?

Knowles argues that visual material allows us to see unspoken ways in which race and ethnicity are lives in this postcolonial space, through unmarked distances and silent intimacies that structure how race is made and experienced. Like Twine, Knowles insists on the partial and staged nature of the images she uses, and on the ways in which both seeing and photography are social practices, as well as techniques. Knowles notes that photos can be used to 'stage' race, and give it an ontological validity centred on the body, and that therefore theorization is integral to the way we take and interpret photographic images, either to reaffirm or to contest racial knowledge.

Embracing reflexivity

In order to address fully the nature of interrelations in the interview, interviewers must also recognize their own ideological frameworks, research tools and practices through reflexivity. But some aspect of social identity and our positions we are not conscious of, and so remain beyond, the reflexive grasp. Ethnic minority researchers have no authority on interpretation and no research is innocent of bias, evasion and selective interpretation. In research where racialized commonalities are identified between researchers and research participants, Gunaratnam among others argues that such constructions can pose particular analytical dangers for minoritized researchers, by obscuring differences in power relations and in the nuances of difference (2003: 7). This recognition of the mutual constitution of embodied experience and social discourse can be problematic for qualitative researchers, particularly if we are concerned with breaking out of circular arguments and those arguments in which researchers are positioned as being outside of the flows between experience and discursive contexts. She argues for a radical reflexivity in research that involves rigorous attention to explicating ways in which research participants and researchers are socially situated (Haraway 1988), at the same time as making our research accountable to the past (Gatens and Lloyd 1999). The idea that research is a part of social and historical relations, and produces rather than simply reflects what we are researching, is encapsulated in the conceptualization of research as a *discursive practice*.

Gunaratnam (2003: 7) argues that conceptualizing research on race as discursive practice opens up analytical opportunities for researchers to interrogate their own current understandings, interests and research practices, and asks how these might be part of what Levine has called 'epistemology as political control' (2000: 17). This is important for three reasons:

1. It challenges a view of research as an unlocated and transparent reflection of some pre-existing, stable reality.
2. It makes our analyses more complex as the research task becomes one in which we need to make sense of knowledge as an emergent property of the interaction between and among differently constituted and located individuals, who include the researcher (Hemmings 2002).
3. It situates our knowledge claims in relation to historical and social relations.

Conclusion

Gunaratnam (2003: 81) advocates three analytical moves that are aimed at identifying and challenging some main assumptions about the nature of interracial encounters in qualitative research. These can be used by any researcher of race in formulating a strategy for dealing with difficulties likely to be encountered in indepth interviewing.

1. A move away from the clear distinction between the social and the technical in methodological practices.

   Following the work of Latour (1983; 1987) in his studies of the natural sciences, a theme that weaves in and out of my analysis is how particular methodological practices, such as ethnic matching, can be seen as 'inscription devices' that aim to simplify and codify the complexity and contingency of difference into unambiguous, predictable and apparently manageable processes.
   (Gunaratnam 2003: 81)

2. A move away from the reification of 'race' and ethnicity in frozen categories and also from giving primacy to race and ethnicity within interview dynamics. This point challenges the interpretation and reading of interview dynamics through one category of difference, and it engages with the postcolonial and multi-cultural realities of hybridity and hypheanated identities (see Song and Parker 1995).

   A failure to recognize the complexity of race in literature means it naively assumes race can be matched. Most people occupy a mixed identity. Gunar-atnam (2003: 81) presents a more complex reality of ethnicity and culture than the one constructed in the methodological literature that fails to acknowledge and engage with what Hall has referred to as the 'places of incommensurability' marked by hybridity (2000: 227).

3   An interrogation and troubling of the binarism of racial and ethnic categories that operate to produce rigid boundaries between different 'races'/ethnicities. Such binaries serves to obscure differences within racialized/ethnicized groups through discourses of commonality, and can position difference as something that cannot be of value in examining and learning from research encounters.

Conducting research in and with communities of another culture can be challenging. Careful selection of methodological approaches is a critical step. Such research requires considerable time, both onsite and in preparation before the data collection begins. The prime focus of the time spent should be on the development of a trusting relationship with the community as a whole and on subsequent trusting relationships with the individuals being asked to share their knowledge and experiences. The researcher needs to develop working relationships with community members. People in the community need to know who the researcher is before they will trust them with information about their lives. This will take time, and real evidence on the part of a researcher of the wish to live in both worlds (Deloria 1991). Humility and generosity should be evident in all of the actions of the researcher while involved in research with communities of color.

Further reading

Emmison, M. (2004) The conceptualization and analysis of visual data, in D. Silverman (ed.), *Qualitative Research: Theory, Method and Practice*, 2nd edn. London: Sage, pp. 246–5. This offers a good critical overview of visual methodology.

Gubrium, J. F. and Holstein, J. A. (eds) (2002) *Handbook of Interview Research*. Thousand Oaks, CA: Sage. This is a thematic and encyclopaedic collection of state of the art descriptions of different approaches interviewing. The *Handbook* covers the theoretical, technical, analytical and representational issues relating to interview research,

Holstein, J. A. and Gubrium, J. F. (1995) *The Active Interview*. Thousand Oaks, CA: Sage. This describes the active interview in greater depth. It provides extensive illustration of the interactional, interpretive activity that is part and parcel of all interviewing.

Kvale, S. (1996) *InterViews*. London: Sage. This is an introduction to qualitative research interviewing. The book frames the issues in terms of the active view presented here.

Silverman, D. (ed.) (2004) *Qualitative Research: Theory, Theory and Practice*, 2nd edn. London: Sage.

Silverman, D. (2001) *Interpreting Qualitative Data: Methods for Analysing Talk, Text and Interaction*. London: Sage.

Wetherell, M. and Potter, J. (1992) *Mapping the Language of Racism: Discourse and the Legitimation of Exploitation*. London and New York: Harvester and Columbia University Press.

Notes

This chapter does not deal with difference in language between researchers and research participants (issues around interpretation and translation) in any detail in this chapter; others have done this effectively elsewhere (for a discussion of language in cross cultural interviews and an overview of some of the literature, see Ryen 2002). However, this is clearly an area that has direct and complicated implications, not only for questions of access, communication and meaning in interracial research but also for patterns of racialization in employment within the social sciences, and for relationships between differently racialized researchers (see Song and Parker 1995; Marshall et al. 1998; Jaschok and Jingjun 2000). But it is important to bear in mind that you don't have to be of the same race to speak the same language.

1   However, as Payne (2007) points out, this is more the case in the British context than in the American.
2   Qualitative research is constituted by a broad range of research methods and although indepth interviewing will be focused on here it is useful to appreciate that it consists of a wide range of methodology including observations, texts, talk, visual data and interviews (Silverman (2004) gives good coverage of all of these). What they all share is a theoretical/ epistemological perspective which sees that the best way of accessing knowledge about the social world is to get to understand the way life is experienced by social actors.

5 Locating 'race' in social research

This chapter is concerned with how a race researcher locates 'race' in their research. Collected data typically do not speak for themselves, a researcher has to employ some method of analysis to make them talk. This chapter focuses upon the 'problem' of how we can analyse racialized identifications and how we can address 'race' in accounts where it is not talked about in direct ways, or where it is embedded and seems invisible. In this regard, the chapter addresses a very basic and general analytical concern – how can we approach the analysis of 'race' in the research participants' accounts? How do we find raced meanings, identifications and interpretations in what our research field is telling us? Among the methodological and practical issues that will be explored here is, how does one avoid bringing one's own 'race thinking' to a research project?

The process of achieving understanding of what you have found through analysis and interpretation can be difficult and highly technical. This chapter will present some key difficulties a race researcher is likely to face and how strategies can be devised, drawing on others work to help overcome them. This chapter builds on the preceding chapters of the book. Accordingly, it will look at finding race through analytical techniques in survey research and interviews.

Introduction

Some race researchers would say that race issues are everywhere and thus unavoidable in any piece of social research. However, the nature of its social construction may mean that it is sometimes more apparent than at other times, and more influential than at other times. Ien Ang (1996) has suggested that processes of racialization can be frustratingly subtle and elusive, rendering them difficult to uncover, analyse and challenge.

It is difficult to know when and how race is present in a research situation or, even more difficult, just how significant it is. The fact that some research is done on race and some not would suggest that its influence and presence is isolated to a few aspects of social life. Some researchers do not mention it so they must not find it an issue in their research experience. Some aspects of social research have been done with very little attention given to race. There is clearly an issue here of whether a researcher not sensitized to race would see it even when present and whether a researcher looking for race issues will find them even when they are not present. Many would argue that the point of social research is to make apparent and make connection between things that otherwise appear invisible.

This book works on the assumption that the researcher is interested in locating race and provides tools for doing so. It builds on the understanding of race developed in the previous chapters, of race as a social construction.

If race is understood as a major social force that is an important background noise, it is seen to be present in most people's lives. When researching race explicitly one can develop ways of viewing and analysis to explore how it is experienced and its significance.

Locating race: combining Knowles and Higginbotham

The theoretical and analytical approach advocated by Higginbotham (1992) and Knowles (2001) has been very influential among recent race researchers (e.g., Gunaratnam 2003: 25). This chapter will outline how they provide a framework for formulating strategies of locating race and some practical methodological advice.

Higginbotham's (1992) idea that race can be read as a 'metanarrative' that can be both hypervisible and invisible in its intersections with other social differences is an important way researchers can make sense of the presence of race in any research encounter.

Higginbotham suggests that:

> Race serves as a 'global sign', a 'metalanguage', since it speaks about and lends meaning to a host of terms and expressions, to myriad aspects of life that would otherwise fall outside the referential domain of race. By continually expressing overt and covert analogical relationships, race impregnates the simplest meanings we take for granted. It makes hair 'good' or 'bad', speech patterns 'correct' or 'incorrect'. It is, in fact, the apparent overdeterminacy of race in Western culture ... that has permitted it to function as a metalanguage in its discursive representation and construction of social relations. Race not only tends to subsume other sets of social relations, namely gender and class, but it blurs and disguises, suppresses and negates its own complex interplay with the very social relations it envelops.
>
> (Higginbotham 1992: 255)

This is a valuable tool in exploring the 'slippery' contradictions of 'race' that Winant has referred to as 'an absent presence, a present absence' (1994: 267).

It enables researchers to approach the interpretation of accounts in which racialized identifications are embedded, but also to address the limitations of analysis in attending to what Derrida (1976) has called 'differance', which refers to both difference and deferral in the construction of meaning. Analysis using Higginbotham's (1992) framework will expose the incomplete and imperfect relations between analysis and lived experience, or what Bourdieu (1990) has called the differences between analytical and practical 'logic'. By this, he means how the very dynamic nature of the meanings and the 'doing' or 'race' in accounts of lived experience can often defy analytical description.

Higginbotham's (1992) approach has been invaluable in examining and accounting for the complexities and nuances of the operation of racial categories in interview data. In broad terms, this theory, derived from Barthes (1972), can be seen as part of 'racial formation theory' (see Omi and Winant 1994; Winant 1994). In racial formation theory, race is theorized as a socially constructed and unstable dynamic of meanings that is produced and negotiated at 'macro' social levels and through individual experience.

A second approach researchers have found useful in trying to locate race in their research data is the analytical approach suggested by Knowles (2001) of disassembling 'race', by examining the ways in which it acquires meaning through different narrative themes in accounts of individual lives. This dissembling should occur along the lines of the (1) personal; (2) structural; and (3) global. This would then deliver units to analyse in which the narratives of individuals can be understood as lived experienced and grounded in relation to other social difference. Combining these approaches is not new and has been done successfully elsewhere (Gunaratnam 2003). Now, it is important to look at the methods that have been used which allow for an articulation of the Higginbotham (1992) and Knowles (2001) framework.

These two approaches allow an appreciation of how different social positions will affect the types of racism community's encounter, their capacity to resist, and how they make sense of their experiences. Race is 'smuggled' into most other social relations (Bourdieu 1984: 102).

It is important to recognize the constrained negotiation and contestation of racialized discourses, identifications and particular power relations. As Knowles suggests, such recognition is important because it can point to individual variation within racialized identifications and to the unevenness of racism, serving to disturb existing typologies of 'race':

> Consideration of individual lives ... brings endless variation to racial categories making it possible to take into account important differences between occupants of the same categories. In trying to explain why racism works so unevenly – why are some the targets of racial violence and others excluded from certain jobs – sociologists have been preoccupied with getting their categories 'right' ... without seriously considering the individual lives composing those categories or the conditions in which race is acquired in the living of lives.
>
> (Knowles 1999: 130)

This chapter builds on the central tension in research on race identified earlier, that is the tension of recognizing that the meanings of 'race' and ethnicity are dynamic and contingent, while also recognizing that many researchers have to fix these meanings at some points in the process of doing empirical research. This chapter will touch on the epistemological and ethical challenges of recognizing and working with ambiguities of meaning in a context of shifting interactional, embodied and social power relations. There are different aspects of this tension, some which can be exposed by examining the production of noticeable insecurities of meaning in researching across difference, and how such areas of ambiguity have been seen as undermining the quality of research interactions and the 'data' generated through them.

Survey methods

Surveys on race as argued earlier are used to find patterns among large populations. This analysis relies on race being an independent variable and having a relationship to other dependent variables. This relationship is explored to describe patterns. For example, a race researcher might argue that black minority boys are more likely to be excluded from school than white or Asian boys. This expresses a relationship between two variables: the race of young boy and the exclusion. Social researchers use the term 'covariation' to describe a general pattern of correspondence. Various quantitative methods can be used to assess the strength of their correspondence. Social researchers calculate correlation in order to assess the strength of a pattern of covariation.

Some variables (called independent or causal variables) may be defined as causes, and others (called dependent or outcome variables) may be defined as effects in a given analysis. The dependent variable is the phenomenon the investigator wishes to explain; independent variables are the factors that are used to account for the variation in the dependent variable. Thus although a survey may not allow much space for respondents to talk about race, if it can get them to identify to a socially recognized category and then collects data about the level of employment, for instance, it can allow an important insight into the racial segregation of the education sector and employment market. The strength of such findings in the US has led to many researchers asserting that a racial hierarchy exists, in which white, Asian, Latino and black people occupy different vantage positions.

In the US, quantitative research is popular but it does run the risk of creating an obstacle between the researcher and audience through the technical nature and complexity of analyses undertaken. Such research addresses key theoretical issues, but not in a way that is easily accessible. Examples include comparative analysis of the position of black and white immigrants in the US (Lieberson 1980) and Lieberson's (1985) methodological reflections upon the complexity of causal analysis in this area; the use of census data to throw light on US experience (Lieberson and Waters 1988); the study of racialization and racism in US politics (Sears et al. 2000). Such studies are testimony to the continuing liveliness of the fields of racial and ethnic studies, but also to barriers that methodology can sometimes erect in communicating the results of sociological research. They also reflect different technical standards between the US and some parts of European social science (Goldthorpe 2000).

Case study: Hierarchies of race

Song (2004) writes that many of the difficulties of trying to find race in social research is in the way that it is theorized. Frequently races are essentialized and seen as basically the same. So black and Asian groups experience race in the same way and experience racial prejudice in similar ways. This being the case, when we try and find 'race' we should try and devote some time to the way the specific group we are studying may experience social existence and devise a project accordingly. This is important not only for us as researchers but also so that it serves a purpose. Of course this will depend on a society's idea of race.

Song (2004: 172) observes that 'while the concept of racial hierarchy has been used liberally in many US studies of race, it is less commonly used in Britain'. She is interested in the question of 'whether or not assertions of racial hierarchy were legitimate or untenable hierarchies of oppression'. The question of whether some groups are worse off than others is highly pertinent at a time when there is growing recognition of multiple forms of racism and racial oppression. What makes the concept of racial hierarchy so compelling is that it is suggestive of an *overall* picture of how different groups fare in multi-ethnic societies. There is little doubt that racial inequalities exist in Britain and the US, but with a few notable exceptions (see Twine 1998; Bonilla-Silva 1999; Kim 1999; Feagin 2000), there is little discussion of what, exactly, are racial hierarchies, and how they operate.

Song (2004: 172–3) in discussing the notion of racial hierarchies for example notes 'systems of ethnic and racial stratification have differed historically, not only in terms of the groups involved, but also the complexity and the magnitude of the distinctions made between groups (see Shibutani and Kwan 1965; Loewen 1971; Almaguer 1994; Twine 1998). While there is considerable agreement about the persistence of white power, privilege and racism (see Sears et al. 2000), the question of which groups do not constitute disadvantaged ethnic minority groups is now more contested and less clear, in comparison with the past. Groups themselves, including White Americans and Britons, are contesting dominant narratives about the existing racial order.

Although the US and Britain have in common the shifting ways in which ideas of 'race' and racial oppression feature in these societies, as well as the emergence of a 'white backlash', British debates about racial inequality and disadvantage differ from those in the US. One aspect of the British debate that especially interested Song (2004) was the assertion by some British analysts that an overarching racial hierarchy, in which groups are placed in a top–down fashion to indicate their relative degree of privilege or disadvantage, was intellectually and politically unacceptable. A key implication of such an argument was that white ethnic minorities, such as Jewish and Irish people, were not necessarily more privileged or less disadvantaged than non-white ethnic minorities such as African Caribbean and South Asian Britons. One would be hard pressed to find a US sociologist who would make such a claim about the status of white ethnic minorities in the US.

It is important to recognize the way that analysis of survey data has allowed researchers to develop a greater understanding of the diversity of inequality experienced by different races. Regional differences are also possible in the treatment of black and Asian groups by white groups, as indicated in Ray and Smith's (2000) study. As Brah (1996) notes, minorities are positioned not only with respect to majorities but also to one another.

Case study

Lindley's (2002) research sought to explore whether race or religion was more important in impact on the employment and earnings of Britain's ethnic communities. Until the 2001 census it was difficult to analyse. What Lindley's research demonstrates is the wealth of information a survey based resource can have. Brown's (2000) work provides evidence that religion is an important determinant of economic activity among Britain's South Asians. He demonstrates significant differences between Indian Hindus, Sikhs and Muslims, and shows Pakistani and

Bangladeshi Muslims to be the most disadvantaged in terms of unemployment of all the South Asian religious groups.

The Fourth National Survey of Ethnic Minorities (FNSEM) was conducted in 1994 by the Policy Studies Institute to investigate the social and economic conditions of the ethnic minorities of England and Wales. The survey over sampled those electoral wards that contained a high percentage of ethnic minorities. The survey contains information on 2867 whites and 5196 non-whites aged 16 and over. Ethnic groups are black Carribeans, Indians, Pakistanis, Bangladeshis, African Asians and Chinese (black Africans were not included). It is possible to distinguish between those born in the UK and those born on ethnic group, as the FNSEM provides information both on ethnic group and on family origin. The survey also provides information concerning the religion of the respondent. The categories are Muslim, Hindu, Sikh, Christian, Buddhist, Jain, Rastafarian, Jewish, Parsi/Zorashia, other religion and no religion.

She discusses how categories can be created to disentangle racial and ethnic effect in an attempt to measure each separately. For example Hindus can be divided into two groups, Indians and African Asians. Her analysis shows how race can be connected to other variables in survey research like religion. She found that Hindu women and men from Africa and India were doing the best in terms of employment and earning profiles and Muslim women, then men from Pakistan and Bangladesh, doing the worst.

Pause for reflection

How would you go about doing a comparative studying of the disadvantages experienced by two racial minority groups?

It seems very important, when analysing survey data, to know the society in which you are doing your research. This does not necessarily have to be limited to the national stage. Each locality in each nationstate has a specific narrative of race to tell (see for example Kandelwal 2002; and Shukla 2005). This will let you know the socio-economic demographics that are important to contextualizing your study. It will also tell you about the racial groups that have historically settled and moved from the area. Each locality has a different set of 'races'.

If races are socially constructed it is this sort of research which will enable you to see how different groups have been differently depicted, how this has changed and how this is reflective of broader social changes. Comparisons of British and American Asian and black people offer a good case study here (Loury et al. 2005). Religion has emerged as something from this analysis. It could be argued that 'Muslims' are in the post-September 11 context are being subjected to racial hatred. What complicates this is that Asian people are seen as Muslims in the British context, where in the American context it is Arab people. In Britain commonality until recently has been stressed among racial minorities as compared to the white majority. The break down of this binary has opened up new spaces for locating race. Sivanandan (1982) and Solomos (2003) have seen the occupation that racial immigrants occupied as giving them a commonality. Modood (in Modood et al. 1997) has pointed to the significance of religion among Asians and the dynamics of 'cultural racism'. In order to research what this broadening of racism means we have to think about how each racial group is prejudged and excluded (Cohen 1996; Hickman 1998). As mentioned earlier by Song (2004), while many British analysts acknowledge that each of these racisms has its own specific history and characteristic features, the implication of such a wide-ranging list of racisms, discussed together, is that they are somehow equivalent and comparable. By comparison, the coupling of anti-Jewish and anti-African racisms would rarely appear in US studies, for the dominant understanding there is that such disparate forms of racism are not equivalent.

Pause for reflection

Consider the advantages and disadvantages of using the following classifications of racial identification in both qualitative and quantitative research: white, black, Asian, Chinese.

- Do you think they are creating boundaries where perhaps none exist?
- By asking these questions are you engendering an awareness of race among your respondents which would not otherwise have occurred?

Qualitative location

In the last few decades, sociological researchers have adopted more qualitative versions of content analysis. These have been influenced by semiotics, which is the study of signs and codes. Semiotics argues that signs and symbols underpin all forms of behaviour and language. Consequently, they are part and parcel of culture and their meaning is learnt and communicated through socialization. Semiotics aims to uncover the hidden meanings that lay behind the use of particular words or images. Signs are said to be made up of two parts: the signifier or denotation and the signified or connotation. The signifier is quite simply what we can see or hear, whereas the signified is its meaning (i.e., what it symbolizes). Semiotics note that objects often present things other than themselves. For example, the signifier 'house' denotes a property in which people live but it also has a range of symbolic or connotative meanings, including 'home', 'family', 'security' and 'financial investment'. This type of analysis would be particularly useful in the analysis of the visual material discussed in Chapter 4.

'Turn to language'

Over the last 20 years research methodologies that take language as their prime analytical site have flourished (e.g., discourse analysis, narrative analysis and conversation analysis). Within this genre there are now some classic studies of 'race' and racism. Wetherell and Potter's (1992) study of the discourses of Pakeha (white New Zealanders), for example, indicates how everyday discourses serve to legitimate racist and exploitative social relations while maintaining liberal discourses of advocating respect and tolerance for cultural difference. More recent studies, for example Augoustinos et al. (1999), also concur.

The most popular methodologies that give primacy to language are discourse analysis, narrative analysis and conversational analysis. Over the past two decades these approaches have made important contributions to the study of race and racism. It has allowed an understanding into new racism (Barker 1981), which is argued to be more subtle then overt racism.

A focus on rhetoric, argumentation, 'commonsense' and thinking as cultural products has enabled insights into the widespread 'norm against prejudice' (Billig 1991) and how it functions in everyday life. Billig argues that the unacceptable attitude towards prejudice are manifest in phrases people use in contemporary society such as 'I'm not prejudiced/racist, but . . .' to cast prejudiced attitudes in non-prejudiced terms (see Barker 1981). Language can reveal much about what people think, how they think they ought to think.

This relatively new qualitative language approach that is frequently characterized as the 'turn to language' is extremely useful in locating race in interview accounts. Language-based approaches have helped with the understanding of how everyday discourses of respect and tolerance for cultural difference operate while legitimating racist and exploitative social relations. They have also demonstrated the complexity and contradiction common to racialized accounts. Phoenix (2004: 51), however, also cautions that 'despite the contribution of language-based approaches, some researchers argue that they are necessarily limited since "there are things that can't be said". Her chapter thinks that it seems appropriate to draw on psychoanalytical concepts in the analysis of language.

Interview analysis

The desire of many researchers to treat interview data as more or less straightforward 'pictures' of an external reality can fail to understand how that 'reality' is being represented in words (Silverman 2004: 4).

Holstein and Gubrium (2004: 4) show us how a focus on story and narrative structure demands that we recognize that both interview data and interview analysis are *active* occasions in which meanings are produced. This means that we ought to view research 'subjects' not as stable entities but as actively constructed through their answers. Indeed Holstein and Gubrium's telling phrase, describing both interviewee and interviewer as 'practitioners of everyday life', reinforces this. Using examples from studies, we can look at where the interpretative practices which generate the 'hows' and the 'whats' of experience as aspects of reality that are constructed in collaboration with the interviewer to produce a 'narrative drama'.

Tape recording interviews, if possible, is a good methodological device because it enables you to listen freely. Keeping in contact with the research respondents is useful, so that you may be able to clarify meanings or ask them to read and check whether you have misinterpreted what they were saying.

Looking for stories

Narrative based methods (Chamberlayne et al. 2000; Hollway and Jefferson 2000; Wengraf 2001). These methods suggest that stories based upon events in peoples lives (rather than opinions, justification and generalizations) provide valuable analytical opportunities for understanding the complexity of accounts of lived experiences. This is because stories can be less open to conscious rationalization. Stories are theorized as holding an unconscious logic and form (a 'gestalt'), through which meanings, emotions and identifications can be expressed in complicated ways, which can sometimes be beyond the conscious control of research participants.

Conversation analysts

Silverman (2004: 48) notes that conversation analysts usually study social interactions by constructing and analysing transcripts made from audio and video recordings of the social interactions. The transcripts are fine-grained representations of the interactions that often include notations indicating the length and placement of pauses, simultaneous talk by interactants, speakers' intonation, words that are stressed or elongated by speakers and the direction of interactants' gazes. Because interactants might take any of these aspects of social interactions into account in responding to others' utterances or in moving the interactions in new directions, they are relevant to conversation analysts' analyses of how social realities are interactionally constructed, sustained and changed.

Methods of collection

Regarding the concern of making one's research credible, we can discuss how qualitative research can seek to offer reliable and valid descriptions. Good transcripts of audio-recorded interactions can maintain the reliability of the data.

It is important to consider what the tape can't record (e.g., appearance, expression, environment). Tapes do not include all aspects of the interaction, you need to think about what to record, the technical quality of recordings and the adequacy of transcripts. Validity questions should also be discussed via the tool available in the conversational analysis methods (e.g., validation through 'next turn' as well as the conventional 'deviant case-analysis').

Discourse analysis

There are many different approaches to discourse analysis, however 'what they share in common is a decisive break with a view of language as a transparent or reflective medium – epi-phenomenal and after the fact' (Wetherell and Edley 1998: 164). The emphasis upon language thus shifts attention away from the individual to the meanings within discourse and to the power relations such meanings construct and negotiate (Willott 1998).

This focuses on how language, both spoken and written, is used in social contexts. The main concern is to recognize the regularities in language – what patterns are there, what repertoires participants have, etc.

Discourse analysis is a way of analysing naturally occurring talk (Potter, in Silverman 2004: 5). It is to focus on how reality is locally constructed; discourse analysis (DA) shares many concerns with conversational analysis (CA). John Heritage (2004) presents an accessible introduction to how conversation analytical methods can be used in the analysis of institutional talk.

While no consensus exists on what discourse analysis is (Potter in Silverman 2004), I have found the definition advocated in the work of Potter (in Silverman 2004) and others are most useful in researching race:

> Discourse analysis . . . is characterized by a meta-theoretical emphasis on anti-realism and constructionism . . . it emphasizes the way versions of the world, of society, events and inner psychological worlds, are produced in discourse. On the one hand this leads to a concern with participants' constructions and how they are accomplished and undermined; and, on the other, it leads to a recognition of the constructed and contingent nature of the researchers' own versions of the world. Indeed, it treats realism, whether developed by participants or researchers, as a rhetorical production that can itself be decomposed and studied.
>
> (Potter in Silverman 2004: 202; see also Gergen 1994;
> Potter 1996; Edwards et al. 1998)

As a complement to this, there is an emphasis on reflexivity.

Foucault (1979b) uses the term 'discourse', analysing more than language. The term also includes the assumptions, logics and modes of articulation associated with particular uses of language. Discourses provide persons with coherent interpretive frameworks and discursive practices for constructing different social realities within which particular kinds of people reside, relationships prevail and opportunities are likely to emerge. We enter into discourses as we go about the practical activities of our lives. The discourses are conditions of possibility that provide us with the resources for constructing a limited array of social realities, and make other possibilities less available to us.

While most applications of Foucault's perspective are analyses of historical texts, most famously Said (1978) applies it to work on Orientalism. Merry's (1990) and Conley and O'Barr's (1990) studies show that these issues may also be studied by using interviews, observational techniques and tape recorded data in a contemporary context. Whatever the form of data, Foucauldian discourse studies involve treating the data as expressions of culturally standardized discourses that are associated with particular social settings. Foucauldian researchers scrutinize their data, looking for related assumptions, categories, logics and claims – the constitutive elements of discourses. They also analyse how different (even competing) discourses are present in social settings; how related social settings may involve different discourses, the political positions of setting members to articulate and apply discourses to concrete issues, persons and events. Jackson's (2001) Harlemworld draws upon Foucauldian discourse studies to analyse Harlem(world) as a place within New York City and as a symbol of African American history and culture. His study shows how people use mundane methods (performances) to cast themselves as members of particular races.

Case study: Analysing racism through discourse analysis

Van Dijk (1993), in a multidisciplinary research programme on discourse and racism carried out in Amsterdam, studied the ways majority group members write and talk about minorities in, for example, everyday conversation/discourse, text-books, news reports, parliamentary debates, and academic and corporate discourse. These analyses have focused on the following major questions:

1   How exactly do members or institutions of dominant white groups talk and write about ethnic or racial minorities?

2   What do such structures and strategies of discourse tell us about under-lying ethnic and racial prejudices, ideologies or other social cognitions about minorities?

3   What are the social, political and cultural contexts and functions of such discourse about minorities? In particular, what role does this play in the development, reinforcement, legitimation and, hence, reproduction of white group dominance?

He argues that the relevance of discourse analysis to the study of racism lies in the study of the discursive reproduction of racism through text and talk provides insight into the relations between various structures of text and talk on minorities on the one hand, and the mental, socio-cultural and political conditions, effects or functions – that is, various 'contexts' – of the reproduction of racism on the other hand.

The study of racism and discourse shows how various grammatical structures, may express or signal the perspectives and ethnic biases of white group speakers. The study of history is largely based on the many types of discourses (stories or documents) from and about the past, including those about race and ethnic events and relations. A detailed discourse analysis of such historical texts allows us to make inferences about otherwise inaccessible attitudes and socio-cultural contexts of racism in the past.

Case study: Finding race in discourse analysis

The way race is currently produced among established immigrant communities vis-à-vis new comers is the focus of Trondman's study. In her study of trying to understand how young people made sense of, challenged or inhabited racialized categories in their everyday lives of young Swedes, Trondman (2006) explored how the social production of 'the immigrant' works to structure their perceptions and experiences. An indepth ethnographic account makes visible both the workings of a 'racial grammar' of 'the immigrant' and the contradictions of how this grammar is played out in the 'dilemmas' faced by 'Swedish' and 'immigrant' young people. For

Trondman discourse analysis is the method by which race can be located in these narratives. It is argued that the grammar, arising in complex external structural and historical processes, is internalized as an 'ingrained stigma' and 'partial truths' that are performed and reproduced at the level of experience and interaction. Her analysis of discourse allowed her to uncover the layered meanings behind the word 'immigrant'. It can mean born abroad or born in Sweden but to foreign born parents. But as Cecilia, one of Trondman's respondents makes clear (2006: 433),

> the problem is that she knows the classification 'immigrant' has another meaning that permeates everyday life in Sweden, namely that *to be an 'immigrant' is to be a representation of social problems*. Thus, it is entirely possible to be an immigrant (to have emigrated and immigrated) without being an 'immigrant' (connoting social problems).

What this second case study of discourse analysis shows us is that 'race' is constructed through continual negotiation of personal, interactional and social dynamics. It also shows how social discourses can have effects upon experience and can also be questioned and contradicted by experience. As Wuthnow suggests: 'While hegemonic representations may categorise and define, there is always resistance to these definitions, and it is the subjective agency embodied in this resistance which constitutes the possibility for oppositional discourses' (2002: 194). Discourse analysis allows a way forward for Gunaratnam (2003) between using poststructuralist critiques of essentialism in research, while also seeking to legitimate the everyday 'situated voices' (Lewis 2000). This approach recognizes the dynamic constitution of the meanings of 'race' and ethnicity through social discourse and through the subjective investments of individuals (see Brah 1996; Hall 1996). It recognizes that social (dominant) discourses are enmeshed in lived experience and institutional and social power relations that have emotional, material and embodied consequences for individuals and for groups. In this sense, I do not theorize social discourses as being outside of experience, subjectivity or bodies; rather, I suggest that social discourses and lived experiences are co-constituted – they intermingle and inhabit one another.

Mats Trondman's (2006) experience of researching race in Sweden demonstrates how the current social-political climate of a national context creates the location of race. It address the way in which the racialized category of 'the immigrant' in Sweden is both inscribed, disrupted and performed in everyday encounters and understandings. He sees the logic of racialized meanings operating as a 'grammar', which constrain the interpretations and locations available to the young people he describes, even as they seek to contest and negate them. Such grammar is, Trondman argues, structurally generated and embedded in the social consciousness of both those positioned as 'immigrants' and as non-immigrants (labels for race), as an ingrained stigma, against which individuals are measured, validated and defined, generating a series of 'dilemmas'. The narrative interview here works to reveal these processes, the intended and unintended consequences, and the struggles through which power is resisted and re-inscribed both at the level of the lived and the imagined.

Narrative interview analysis allows for an exploration of the shifting boundaries of race and ethnicity in contemporary societies. For example, a great deal of research on race focuses on young people. How do young people talk about issues of race in their everyday environments? Attention to the ambiguities of meaning can provide researchers with valuable analytic and ethical insights into the nature and negotiation of social, interactional and biographical difference in research encounters. Though a discussion of a number of studies (for example Back 1996; Phoenix 2000; Alexander 2001; Gunaratnam 2003) researchers have engaged with ethnical concerns and dilemmas, for example through a discussion of a researcher's accountability to the 'refusing subject' (Visweswaran 1997), where loss of meaning can also convey a resistance to a negotiation of the subject positions that are produced and made in the research encounter.

Micro-analysis of interview data

The micro-analysis of interview data involves securing a meaning to the patterns that have been found through techniques like discourse analysis. The process of micro-analysis that has been used by race researchers is derived from the biographical narrative interpretative method (see Wengraf 2001), and involves the use of a 'panel' of people, with very small pieces of interview text (sometimes just one or two words) being presented to them in sequence. Based upon the words given to them, the panel suggest possible meanings and formulate hypotheses about the relationships between the meanings of the words, their relation to events and experiences talked about in the interview (for example, what the words might be referring to and what might come next) and the interview interaction (Rosenthal 1993). Different approaches to micro-analysis can be found in the work of Pittenger and Danehy (1960); Labov and Fanshel (1977); and Scheff (1997).

A difficulty of relying on language

Phoenix (2004) writes that:

> Qualitative research has gained legitimacy in many disciplines and much of this work pays close attention to what people say and write on the understanding that, since meanings are constructed in language, this should be the primary site for understanding social interactions (Potter and Wetherell 1987). This 'turn to language' has influenced all forms of qualitative methodology and generated many debates about epistemology. The resulting methods have produced much insightful and exciting work. However, the application of these methods to research on racism raises a number of tricky issues. For example, are there, as Stephen Frosh et al. (2002) and Hollway and Jefferson (2000) argue, important 'things that can't be said' because the emotions they arouse lead them to be pushed into the unconscious? If so, what are the implications for our understanding of accounts that confirm or deny experiences of racism? In addition, how can large scale demographic data (much favoured by policy makers) contribute to qualitative analyses?

A major concern among social scientists working within language analysis, as a window into understanding race, has been the 'things that can't be said' because they are not part of conscious action or thought:

> It seems to me that while the 'turn to language' has been enormously valuable in attending to the production of (particularly) conscious meanings, there is a danger ... of *reducing* meaning to that which can be narrated, that which can be clearly said ... My view on this is that psychoanalysis show very clearly that there is a point where discourse fails, where language is characterized by its insufficiency rather than its expressive capacity, where what is known in and by a person lies quite simply outside symbolisation.
>
> (Frosh 2002: 134–5)

Psychoanalysis has become increasingly popular among researchers seeking to account for what 'can't be said' (e.g., Rattansi 1994; Walkerdine et al. 2001; Frosh et al. 2002). Hollway (1984, 1989) and Hollway and Jefferson (2000) drew on the ideas of the psychoanalyst, Melanie Klein. Wetherell (1998) is sceptical of the need to turn to psychoanalysis to explain social meaning because she argues that the unconscious is produced in discourse.

Case study of whiteness: Finding race with photographs

White groups are frequently seen as 'the refusing' or difficult subject in race research because they are reluctant to view themselves as having a racial identity.

Photographs are seen as a way of seeing/locating whiteness by advocates like Knowles (2003), using the professional photographic services of Douglas Harper. There are two problems for those who make photographic images as part of an investigation and analysis of race: the selection and arrangement of objects at which the lens is aimed and the theoretical analysis in which the image is rendered. The general invisibility of whiteness means we are anxious about whether we are seeing race or just normal people. Studies have tended to focus on spectacular events, such as football violence, right wing extremism or lynch mobs in the US. A good example of this is Smith's (2004) excellent account of whiteness in the US South during the Jim Crow era. Using archival photographs, she points out that lynching was a celebratory spectacle of whiteness in which people posed in groups or were captured by the lens, smiling, affirming themselves and their place within the racial hierarchies of the South against the black dismembered bodies of their Others. This for some does not tackle it as a normative position. In contrast Knowles's racial analysis of the photographs of white British expatriates in her research is not underwritten by overtly racialized encounters or by spectacles of violence. The photographs that were chosen were expected to reflect the themes that Knowles and Harper thought they were working on.

Case study: Mixed race analysis

Locating race through photographs has enabled Twine (2006) among others to 'see' and thus locate the socio-racial world in which their research subjects operate. An analysis of photographs she argues, can economically and effectively communicate the socio-political stakes for individuals who either inhabit bodies that are perceived as racially ambiguous or who are ambivalent about their racial status.

Twine (2006) employed a model for 'photograph-elicitation interviews' in longitudinal ethnographic research on race and intimacy in her research among British interracial families between 1995 and 2003. Sociologists have used photographs from a wide range of sources in photo-elicitation interviews. They have used archival photographs (Modell and Brodsky 1994); photographs taken by the researcher (Harper 1984; Gold 1986; Burkett 1997); photographs taken by professional photographers working with researchers (Duneier 1999; Knowles 2003); photographs taken by participants in the research (Sprague 1978; Douglas 1998; Harrington and Lindy 1998; Ali 2003); and family snapshots taken by family members (Twine 1998).

She evaluates her use of family photographs in photo-elicitation interviews as a methodological tool, a source of primary data and as evidence for theory. She used photo-interviews as a collaborative methodological tool to clarify and challenge theories that I had developed to explain how white birth mothers of African descent children negotiate their 'racial profiles' in public and private arenas. She analysed a particular case study of one transracial mother who strategically employed family photographs to project respectable 'presentations' of her interracial familial life. She discusses the various ways that photographs can be used in ethnographic research. She uses photographs as a primary source of data, such as a visual record to study the material and social *settings* in which her research subjects live and as evidence for theory. Then she focused on case studies that were particularly useful to illustrate how she employed family photograph albums as a collaborative research tool to theorize how racial and ethnic identities are projected for consumption in the context of racial hierarchies, class inequalities and heterosexual marriage. Among the uses she made were:

1 Employing photographs as a research tool for producing visual records and collecting data about the material world in which people live.
2 Using 'reflexivity' during photo-interviews of the 'racial tours' of an interracial marriage. These photo-elicitation interviews were conducted several years after I had completed racial consciousness and life history interviews and participant observation. She did not then use photo-interviews as 'can-openers' to establish rapport but rather to clarify the differences between what was 'perceived' and what was said in the presence and absence of photographs. Family photo albums (using Smith's ideas 1999, 2003) are a valuable analytical lens to theorize how photographs may be deployed by middle class family members to negotiate racial identities and to project middle class respectability.

She also set goals. From the photo-interviews she wanted to:

1   map the socio-racial fields in which transracial mothers operate.
2   Detect changes in the racial and ethnic structure of the family over time.
3   Identify significant people in her social and familial network.
4   Identify which members of her familial and social network were present at life events such as the birth of children, the baptism of children, the weddings and funerals of family and friends.
5   Identify contradictions and tensions between the themes that occurred repeatedly in private conversations and semi-structured interviews and the content of our conversation during these photo-interviews.

She applies Banks' (2001) analysis that photographs are 'tiny mirror fragments' that provide a partial view of the social fabric of people's lives. Marcus (1998) identifies three contexts in which photographs are read including: (1) the context of the original production of the photograph; (2) subsequent histories of the photographs; and (3) the context in which the social researcher deploys the photographs in the course of an interview.

This type of analysis challenged Twine to re-examine and rethink her earlier analyses of the ways that race intersects with age, occupation, education, marital status and gender hierarchies to structure the lives of white members of interracial families (Twine 1999). She used photographs to examine the racial profiles that transracial parents project and the shifts in their racial logic as they reconcile the gaps between their intimate lives and how they are racialized in the public sphere (Twine 1998).

Case study: Historical documentary analysis

A great deal of literature exists around the use of documents for social research (Scott 1990; Prior 2003, 2004). Prior (2004) emphasizes three specific features of documents as a field for social research: how documentation is produced in socially organized contexts; how documentation is used in everyday organizational action; and how documentation enters into the manufacture of self and identity (produced and manipulated beyond their creator's control). The early discussion of the social embeddedness of racial categories, enables insights into colonialism as an uneven process that operated in differential ways across time and space (Thomas 1994; Young 1995). It is useful to examine how racial categories have been applied to different groups of white people. For example, the British Empire and its domineering expansion, based upon systems of direct and indirect governance, began with Ireland and produced a 'racialisation' of the presumed inferiority of the 'Irish' (Agnew 1999: 98). In an analysis of the letters of the anthropologist Charles Knigsley, written in the 1860s in England, Lorimer (1978) has highlighted how 'scientific' anti-racism, which played upon notions of intelligence, was a significant part of debates about the extension of voting rights.

> **Pause for reflection**
>
> In what ways do contemporary newspaper stories about white immigration and discrimination allow an insight in this racialized group? For example, in what ways are East Europeans documented in popular stories?

Bonnett (1998) in a critical history of the conflation of European and white identities from nineteenth and twentieth century commentaries, has drawn attention to the historical and geographical contingency of whiteness, thereby challenging it as a 'natural', homogenous category. Bonnett's works traces the marginalization and exclusion of Chinese and Middle Eastern white identities in the formation of European racialized whiteness, that was itself further inflected by ethnic, class and gender hierarchies. In addressing English Victorian class relations, Bonnett points to constructions of upper class English people as being 'more white' than those from the working classes.

It is significant that in whiteness studies, the silences of whiteness as a racialized identity have been seen as critical to social and intersubjective power relations. Simpson (1996) has argued that the silences of whiteness serve the purpose of producing a deracialized identity, enabling those categorized as white to ignore, deny or avoid, or forget their racialized subjective and social positioning. The analytical concern with the evasion and the non-manifestation of 'race' and ethnicity through whiteness has thus led to the mapping of new methodological and epistemological terrain, concerned with recognizing and uncovering the ways in which whiteness is produced through its silences and invisibility.

These assumptions not only effect the production of knowledge but also the way we experience research. Initial feelings and evaluations of what had been good or bad interviews with respondents were related to the extent to which questions of 'race' had been referred to explicitly within the accounts. Researchers should explore how the non-manifestation of racial identifications in the accounts of racialized research participants could maintain and/or subvert processes of racialization. For example, if the power of whiteness as a social category and an identity is based upon its silence, can the silence of identity in those marked as racial, signal a disruption of racialized binaries?

Documentary analysis

McDonald (2001: 196) defines documents as: 'Things that we can read and which relate to some aspect of the social world – official reports, for example – but there are also private and personal records such as letters, diaries and photographs, which may not be meant for the public gaze at all'.

Robson (2007: 28) similarly notes

> the term 'document' suggests a printed source of some kind. In research it is usually defined more widely to include photographs, films and other non-written sources. A research project can be based solely on the analysis of

documentary evidence of one form or another (e.g. in historical or literature research). Typical printed or written documents include:

Minutes of meeting of various kinds
Formal and informal records of different bodies
Letters and diaries
Inspection and others reports, and
Electronic documents such as websites.

Documents can form a part of race research in two ways. As the starting point in the selection of one or more key documents from which you can develop your research question. The alternative approach is start from the research question or problem and then locate appropriate documents to analyse.

In recent years a number of researchers have researched 'mixed race' using documents in both historical and contemporary analysis (Ali 2003; Phoenix 2004; Small 2004). Much of this work has focused on 'the experiences of people of mixed African and European origins (usually termed 'mixed race'). Some writers have been concerned with the expressed identities of people of mixed origins (Spickard 1989; Root 1992). Others have been more concerned with institutional experiences, material resources and ideological articulations by dominant groups (Small 1989, 1994). Small, in his research, is concerned with whether they were preferentially treated over black people during nineteenth century slavery in the US. He explores this by looking at the type of work, freedom and treatment by others.

Data sources for historical studies of black populations are difficult to get hold of. So the first difficulty for exploring mixed race experiences was finding an appropriate range of documents. Small found a range of documents were useful, for example (2004: 87): 'manuscript sources from a range of plantations, farms and urban employers, including letters, diaries, wills, memoirs, autobiographies, work routines and 1850 census'.

Small's (2004: 89) use of historical data for sociological race analysis yielded several observations. He argues that

[1.] an extensive literature review is indispensable in order to assess the state of knowledge on the topic, and methodologically for helping locate the key collections of historical documents, and where they are archived (that is where, geographically). This will also tell you the names of the specific collections within the archives. It is then your responsibility to go beyond the collections cited – these are not the universe of all collections relevant to your own project – and to do so by systematically using indexes of various kinds, as well as following some intuitions and unlikely trails. During this preliminary review, and before you get to the archives, you should try to locate substantial data available via microfilm from major libraries, and important plantation collections. You should also contact scholars who have previously worked (or are currently working) on the field and develop good relations with them and with archive staff. This will save you substantial time and money.

[2.] Be critical of the extant concepts, be prepared to reject those that are offensive or inappropriate, to develop your own concepts and defend them.

[3.] When you get to the archives, spend time getting a comprehensive overview of how the various collections are arranged and keep meticulously organized and detailed notes of what is in them. Take photocopies galore, anything you think you might use, and bring them back to home base. Be prepared to spend substantial time following leads of various kinds, and expect that trails that bring you to a deal end are simply par for the course.

[4.] Finally, for the empirically data sets, be sure to review quantitative and qualitative data sets as appropriate, and to cross-check them for important and key issues. You will have to delve into a wide range of sources of various levels of reliability and usefulness over a long period of time, so extensive record keeping is indispensable.

What is apparent from Small's (2004: 90) experience is the conceptualization and formulation of research projects has common elements for many researchers. They, first, always involve a question of theory and of epistemology. A second set of problems has to do with the trials and tribulations of the research process. This is more often a question of practicalities. In both endeavours we are confronted by the finiteness of time. The issue is how to avoid uncritically genuflecting to the conceptualizations of previous generations of scholars (whose concepts and assumptions continue, in many respects, to burden us), and how to escape being swallowed up in the vastness and variety of the resources. There is also the tricky question of how to write up our project. In respect to these questions, a clear methodology – conceptual clarity, the specificity of sources and a definite strategy for accessing them – becomes a device for escaping from the prison of the finiteness of time. But this is not just about making life easy for yourself, these criteria also serve as a device for constructing a story that has authority – it has authority because it has rigour, depth, is systematic and comprehensive.

'For my specific project', Small writes (2004: 90),

> I was unhappy with many of the assumptions in the literature, with some of the key concepts and with the empirical data used to answer the questions. After considerable review of the literature, and collection of data, I was able to offer counter-arguments based on better data. I argue that Blacks of mixed origins certainly enjoyed many privileges and considerable advantage when compared to Blacks presumed to be of unmixed origins. But I found that these have been considerably exaggerated and that, when we take a fuller account of all Blacks of mixed origins and all Blacks, the picture is more complicated.

Among the advantages of using documents as the basis of your analysis of race are: the independence of your research and the documents you are exploring were produced for some other purpose. Second, carrying out your research has no effect on the document itself. Such possible effects, referred to as reactivity, bedevil much research. There is the logical problem that if your research affects the thing researched, then you don't know what the situation would be in the absence of the research.

Among the disadvantages of using documents are the fact that they have been produced for some other purpose; this will almost certainly affect their nature and content.

Historians have been much exercised by the problems of evaluating documentary evidence (see for example Barzun and Graff 2000). Knowing the intended audience for the document gives insights into likely bias. The more you can find out about the context in which the document was produced, and of the characteristics of its writer, the better. The basic rule is never to accept what the document says at face value, but to try to get at why it says what it does.

Conclusion

It is important that the researcher is aware of the tools that are available in analysing his or her collected data. When formulating any research project on race ideally they should be built into the project design. Researchers have typically differed on the way they locate race in their data, in quantitative methods like surveys and qualitative methods like indepth interviewing. Analytical methods such as correlations between variables in survey analysis have enabled researchers to trace powerful patterns between the race of individuals and their experiences of education and employment, for instance. Indepth interviewing language has special significance in locating race. Various methods including discourse analysis have been used to find race in interview narratives.

Further reading

Alexander, C. (2002) *Ethnic and Racial Studies*, Special Edition. This special edition provides a good discussion on different conceptualization of black and Asian people which seems to have been consolidated in the 9/11 and 7/7 contexts.

Holstein, A. J. and Gubrium, J. F. (1995) *The Active Interview*. London: Sage. The volume describes the active interview in greater depth. It provides extensive illustration of the interactional, interpretive activity that is part and parcel of all interviewing.

Ray, L. and Smith, D. (2000) Hate crime, violence and cultures of racism, in P. Iganski (ed.), *The Hate Debate*. London: Profile Books. For the ways that white groups in North America are selective in the racist attitudes they direct towards Asian people.

Silverman, D. (2000) *Doing Qualitative Research*. London: Sage.

Silverman, D. (2001) *Interpreting Qualitative Data: Methods for Analysing Talk, Text and Interaction*, 2nd edn. London: Sage. 'Interviews', chapter 4 of this volume deals with a variety of approaches to interviewing. The chapter considers active interviewing in relation to different approaches, including emotionalism, constructionism, and ethnomethodology.

Song, M. (2004) Racial hierarchies in the USA and Britain: investigating a politically sensitive issue, in M. Bulmer and J. Solomos (eds), *Researching Race and Racism*. London: Routledge, pp. 172–86. This provides an analysis of different races/different forms of racism using an American and British comparison. It is a good overview of how different theoretical heritages have created different epistemological and methodological approaches.

Yin, R. K. (2002) *Case Study Research: Design and Methods*, 3rd edn. London: Sage. A key text on case study design.

6 Conclusion

While this book has argued that social researchers need to appreciate that race is a social and political construction, the investigation into it remains urgent given the realities of racism, discrimination, violence and terror, and these are grounds on which to 'trump our theoretical misgivings' (Alexander 2006: 398). Alexander further argues that:

> It is nevertheless the case that race research has at the same time tended to sideline issues around methodology, practice and politics. Though the majority of empirical work comfortably addresses the methods, settings and subjects/ objects of research – the *hows*, *whens* and *whos* – the more difficult issues of the institutional, personal and political agendas (the whys) generating research, a clear sighted and honest assessment of the dynamics within research encounters (turning the gaze back on the *who* and the *how* within the research) and a reckoning with the consequences of conducting research (the *shoulds*, *what ifs* and *why nots*) remain unconsidered, or pushed uncomfortably to one side.
>
> (2006: 398)

This book has attempted to demonstrate that theory, technique and practical application are inseparable when it comes to carrying out or contemplating research. At all stages, practical research issues and dilemmas are intertwined with questions of the ethics/politics and social theory which underpin them.

This concluding chapter is interested in some future orientated discussion framed along the main sections of the book:

1 *Theoretical and historical issues*. New types of population movements in the West and beyond may mean that the words 'migrant' and 'race' are differentiated and whiteness comes under increasingly close scrutiny. Globalization and particularly the 'war on terror' may create new targets of discrimination – religious minorities. Thus the theoretical context for developing understandings of race will change and researchers will need to work within this new framework.

2 *Methodological terrains*. The boundaries of multiple methods must be engaged with by races researchers. Artificial divides between quantitative and qualitative research are not helpful and things are decidedly more messy. Also this volume has attempted to show that single method based research will inevitably be flawed. Multilevelled research will, as Payne (2007) argues, at least go some way to cancelling each individual method flaws out.

Contemporary researchers are in a privileged age, able to make use of old/new theorization and new technological methodology.

3 *Intellectual climate*. Research practice varies according to national context and so does the conceptualization of race. As societies engage with these, some never

having given it much thought, and some having to revisit aspects of how they understood themselves, it will continue to be an area of research that must be contextualized to be understood. It seems likely that the ways in which race research is thought and done will become a more contested zone.

Continued tensions into the future

There will be a continued tension in the recognition of race as a construction and the need to define it for the purpose of research. Also it will need to defend its usage vis-à-vis other concepts such as ethnicity, as these will be as popular as ever. Moreover there will be pressure to conform to the political agenda, but this will also indicate areas of popular concern. Trends in the funding of research, as discussed earlier, stress the need for social science research to be seen as 'relevant' and 'useful' for addressing 'everyday' concerns – with 'usefulness' being interpreted in relations to the need to build and support policy and practice (Lewis 2000).

Methodological debates

Research on race is and should be related to wider discussions on methodology in sociology. As Crompton (2008) argues, the intellectual divisions that have plagued the subject continue to do so. Similarly, all sociologists focus on 'the social' in some way or other but we are not necessarily expert in each other's specialities. We need not be too concerned, therefore, about the heterogeneity of sociology as an academic discipline. Nevertheless, individual sociologists are still prone to arguing that there is 'one best way' of doing sociology. While race is connected to many other social divisions and there may be a good strategy for researching it in a particular scenario, a researcher should not be constrained by this. For example, while it is connected to other social difference we can still focus on one aspect of race inequality with respectability – though we should be cautious of making it a hyper-specialized type of research (Payne 2007).

As Crompton (2008) argues, a range of methodological expertise is essential for practising sociologists in any field. A range of expertise is required not least because different research problems or topics will require different research methods – there is no 'one size fits all' technique available for doing research. Rejecting conventional research in favour of 'social transactional technologies' (Savage and Burrows 2007) is not the way to go.

Savage and Burrows (2007) argue that in an age of knowing capitalism sociologists have not adequately thought about the challenges posed to their expertise by the proliferation of 'social' transactional data, which are now routinely collected, processed and analysed by a wide variety of private and public institutions. Drawing on British examples they argue that, whereas over 40 years sociologists championed innovative methodological resources, notably the sample survey and the indepth interviews, which reasonably allowed them to claim distinctive expertise to access the 'social' in powerful ways, such claims are now much less secure. They argue that both the sample survey and the indepth interviews are increasingly dated research methods which are unlikely to provide a robust base for the jurisdiction of empirical sociologists on how sociology might respond to this coming crisis through taking up new interests in the 'politics of method'.

This interest in the 'politics of method' involves sociologists renewing their interests in methodological innovation and reporting critically on new digitalization. This draws on the arguments of writers such as Pickstone (2002) and Latour (2005) who argue – for different reasons – that we abandon a sole focus on causality and analysis and embrace instead an interest in description and classification.

Payne (2007), as Crompton concurs, argues that sociological diversification has created 'hyper-specialized' sociologists in subject expertise and methodology, resulting in sociologists knowing more and more about less and less. Exploring multidimensional social life requires knowing about more than one field and having skills in more than one method. An approach based on an integrated view of social divisions and expanded methodological pluralism, in which we moderate our claims to sociological generalization, is proposed as a way forward.

Future categories

Ultimately, all of the discussions in the book hinge on examining and making explicit the different ways in which questions of 'race' and ethnicity are central to all race research. An additional aim of the discussions is to explore how we might produce and develop methodological, epistemological and ethnical practices that, in uncovering and attending to 'race' and ethnicity as socially produced categories, can provide a means of disrupting and challenging the oppressive power relations that can flow from racialized thinking.

The drive towards categorization at the beginning of the twenty first century will continue. This needs to be understood in relation to complicated postcolonial relations that are played out on a global stage and have a localized impact upon our research. But these categories of race need to be challenged by the contemporary race researcher. Race is rarely as neat in social life as categories would suggest.

This is useful to explore in discussions of diasporas and the concept of racial space used to refer to 'the entanglement ... of the genealogies of dispersion with those of "staying put"'. Using England as an example, Brah (1996) suggests that difference is played out and negotiated at many levels so that:

> African-Carribean, Irish, Asian, Jewish and other diasporas intersect among themselves as well as with the entity constructed as 'Englishness', thoroughly re-inscribing it in the process ... in the post-war period this Englishness is con-tinually reconstituted via a multitude of border crossings ... These border crossings are territorial, political, economic, cultural and psychological.
>
> (1996: 209)

It is not that we need more categories, rather that this approach of simple categor-ization does not capture the nuances of race. A researcher, by challenging these cate-gories, aids their transformation. The types of race identification likely to be developed in the coming years will not be the same as those around currently, but they will have a relationship to them. It is not simply about refining categories but about bringing them into line with a changing reality.

It seems that the development of disciples and specialisms has created a division among methodological and theoretical which has not been entirely helpful in the research of race.

This conclusion aims to suggest a few ways forward for the research of race. It advocates, in keeping with the argument throughout the book, an integration of race research with research on other aspects of social life and a multimethod approach. It seems to me that the most important point of any research exercise is that it has some meaning outside the academic community, thus it should deal with issues of social importance, and these rarely occur in the singular, and possible to tackle through one method.

A cursory glance at history would suggest that this preference for singular methods has not always been the case. For example, Gunnar Myrdal's (1944) classic study of race relations in the US, *An American Dilemma: The Negro Problem and Modern Democracy* represents a multidisciplinary and policy orientated interpretative framework that underpinned this forcefully anti-racist synthesis of a large amount of empirical data.

It might be useful to explore classic studies for the research methodologies they employed. In her work on the history of research methods in America before the war, Platt (2005) outlines the methodological creativity, pluralism and experimentation, and the close relationship between social reform oriented social scientists, that characterized the prewar period of research (Platt 2005; see also Bulmer 1997).

The future of race research has to include theoretical, epistemological and methodological bridges being made. For example the concern with new races, like refugees, should be linked to existing British minorities. Methodological plurality and theoretical plurality results in innovation. The solution may be in a healthy balance of reviewing our history and embracing our future.

If we are too specialized we risk a marginalization of our research when it should be done because it has a relevance to wider society not solely for our academic peers. There is a danger of super-specialization where findings will be inaccessible to non-specialist. Indeed as May (2005: 9) argues 'the problem of substantive and theoretical super-specialisation raises the possibility that a shared methodological vocabulary may now be the *only* point of contact'.

As Lauder et al. (2004: 3) note 'sociology needs to develop an approach to research which focuses on fundamental social problems'. This will demand, since the problems are complex, interdisciplinary input (theory and methodological) and the development and appraisal of theories. This seems very daunting and perhaps I can suggest a piecemeal approach as being more appropriate, for example, as this allows consideration of the implications around the conceptualization of a research question, collection of data and analysing of material.

There has been a tendency in race research to concentrate heavily on the theoretical validity of the concept of 'race'. Namely whether it actually exists or not. This can be seen in the recent post-race theoretical discussions. While this volume is not disputing the validity of engaging with theoretical debate, at the very least to understand what we and our contemporaries understand by the concept of 'race' – in the discourse of social research how we operationalize our concepts. It does seem, however, to engage in sterile debate about the existence of race, which tends to be overshadowed by the fact that in everyday life being 'raced' has implications for how you live (or indeed are allowed to live) your everyday life and the types of opportunities and resources you will have access to. Race, this volume asserts, matters because, whether it is real or not, it is acted upon by others as if it is real and thus any other aspects of this discussion becomes less important. I think nearly all the respondents I have interviewed over the years would not care much for this discussion around whether race exists, because for them its existence is indisputable because racism exists. Indeed, as Miles (1986) have argued, it is racism that demarcates race.

If the aim of a social researcher is to enhance social existence then researchers must be able to work with a loose idea around race and a firm idea that they are engaging in an attempt to better people's lives. Theory must be informed by empirical research, indeed theoretical discussions about whether race exists shouldn't take place without being informed by life. A retreat into theory is a mistake, a retreat into action is a danger, the third way is a way empirical/practical research can result in better informed theory.

References

Agnew, J. (1999) *Geopolitics: Re-Visioning World Politics*. New York: Routledge.

Ahmad, W. I. U. and Sheldon, T. (1991) 'Race' and statistics, *Radical Statistics Newsletter*, 48(spring): 27–33.

Ahmad, W. I. U. and Sheldon, T. (1993) 'Race' and statistics, in Hammersley (ed.), *Social Research: Philosophy, Politics and Practice*. London: Sage, pp. 123–4.

Ahmad, F., Modood, T. and Lissenburgh, S. (2003) *South Asian Women and Employment in Britain: Interaction of Gender and Ethnicity*. London: Policy Studies Institute.

Ahmed, S. (2000) *Strange Encounters, Embodied Others in Post-Coloniality*. London: Routledge.

Alexander, C. (1996) *The Art of Being Black: The Creation of Black British Youth Identities*. Oxford: Oxford University Press.

Alexander, C. (2000) *The Asian Gang: Ethnicity, Identity, Masculinity*. Oxford: Berg.

Alexander, C. (2004) Writing race: ethnography and the imagination of the Asian Gang, in M. Bulmer and J. Solomos (eds), *Researching Race and Racism*. London: Routledge.

Alexander, C. (2006) Introduction: mapping the issues, *Ethnic and Racial Studies*, 29(3): 397–410.

Alexander, C. and Knowles, C. (eds) (2005) *Making Race Matter: Bodies, Space and Identity*. Basingstoke and New York: Palgrave Macmillan.

Alexander, J. and Mohanty, C. (eds) (1997) *Feminist Genealogies, Colonial Legacies, Democratic Future*. London: Routledge.

Ali, S. (2003) *Mixed Race, Post Race: Gender, New Ethnicities and Cultural Practices*. Oxford: Berg.

Ali, S. (2004a) Post race, in Ellis Cashmore (ed.), *Encyclopaedia of Race and Ethnic Studies*, pp. 323–5.

Ali, S. (2004b) Reading racialised bodies: learning to see difference, in H. Thomas and J. Ahmed (eds), *Cultural Bodies: Ethnography and Theory*. London: Blackwell.

Ali, S. (2006) Racializing research: managing power and politics? *Ethnic and Racial Studies*, 29(3): 471–86.

Alleyne, B. (2002) *Radicals Against Race: Black Activism and Cultural Politics*. Oxford: Berg.

Almaguer, T. (1994) *Racial Fault Lines*. Berkeley: University of California Press.

Anderson, E. (1990) *Streetwise: Race, Class and Change in an Urban Community*. Chicago: University of Chicago Press.

Anderson, E. (1999) *The Code of the Street: Decency, Violence and the Moral Life of the Inner City*. Chicago: University of Chicago Press.

Anderson, E. ([1976] 2003) *A Place on the Corner*. Chicago: University of Chicago Press.

Anderson, M. (1993) Studying across difference: race, class and gender in qualitative research, in J. Stanfield and R. Dennis (eds), *Race and Ethnicity in Research Methods*. Newbury Park, CA: Sage, pp. 39–52.

Ang, I. (1996) The curse of the smile: ambivalence and the 'Asian' woman in Australia multiculturalism, *Feminist Review*, 52: 36–49.

Aquilino, W. S. (1994) Interview mode effects in surveys of drug and alcohol use: A field experiment, *Public Opinion Quarterly*, 58(2): 210–40.

Asad, T. (ed.) (1973) *Anthropology and the Colonial Encounter*. Atlantic Highlands, NJ: Humanties Press.

Aspinall, P. (2001) Operationalising the collection of ethnicity data in studies of the sociology of health and illness, *Sociology of Health and Illness*, 23(6): 828–62.

Augoustinos, K., Tuffin, M. and Rapley, M. (1999) Genocide or failure to gel? Racism, history and nationalism in Australia, *Discourse and Society*, 10(3): 351–78.

Baca Zinn, M. Chicano family research: conceptual distortions and alternative directions, *Journal of Ethnic Studies*, 7(3): 24–49.

Back, L. (1996) *New Ethnicities and Urban Culture*. London: UCL Press.

Back, L. (2003) Ivory Towers? The academy and racism, in I. Law, D. Phillips and L. Turney (eds), *Institutional Racism in Higher Education*. Stoke-on-Trent: Trentham Books.

Back, L. (2004) Reading and writing research, in C. Seale (ed.), *Researching Society and Culture*. London: Sage.

Back, L. and Solomos, J. (1993) Doing research, writing politics: the dilemmas of political intervention in research on racism, *Economy and Society*, 22(2): 178–99.

Bakhtin, M. (1981) *The Dialogical Imagination*, trans, C. Emerson and A. Holquist. Austin, TX: University of Texas Press.

Banks, M. (1996) *Ethnicity: Anthropological Constructions*. London: Routledge.

Banks, M. (2001) *Visual Methods in Social Research*. London: Sage.

Barker, M. (1981) *The New Racism: Conservatives and the Ideology of the Tribe*. London: Junction Books.

Barker, F., Hulme, P. and Iversen, M. (eds) (1994) *Colonial Discourse/Postcolonial Theory*. Manchester: Manchester University Press.

Barthes, R. (1972) *Mythologies*, trans. A. Lavers. New York: Hill and Wang.

Barzun, J. and Graff, H. (eds) (2000) *The Modern Researcher*, 6th edn. New York: Harcourt Brace Jovanovich.

Bashi, V. (1998) Racial categories matter because racial hierarchies matter: a commentary, *Ethnic and Racial Studies*, 21(5): 959–68.

Bauman, Z. (1991) *Intimations of Postmodernity*. London: Routledge.

Bauman, Z. (1999) *Culture as Praxis*. London: Sage.

Bendle, M. F. (2002) The crisis of 'identity' in high modernity, *British Journal of Sociology*, 48(3): 320–40.

Benson, S. (1996) Asians have culture, West Indians have problems: discourse of race and ethnicity in and out of anthropology, in T. Ranger, Y. Samad and O. Stuart (eds), *Culture, Identity and Politics*. Aldershot: Avebury.

Bhabha, H. (1994) *The Location of Culture*. London: Routledge.

Bhatt, C. (2004) Contemporary geopolitics and 'alterity' research, in M. Bulmer and J. Solomos (eds), *Researching Race and Racism*. London: Routledge.

Bhattacharyya, G., Gabriel, J. and Small, S. (2002) *Race and Power: Global Racism in the Twenty-First Century*. London: Routledge.

Bhopal, K. (2001) Researching South Asian women: issues of sameness and difference in the research process, *Journal of Gender Studies*, 10(3): 279–86.

Billig, M. (1991) *Ideology and Opinions: Studies in Rhetorical Psychology*. London: Sage.

Billig, M., Condor, S., Edwards, D. et al. (1988) *Ideological Dilemmas: A Social Psychology of Every Day Thinking*. London: Sage.

Blahna, D. J. and Black, K. S. (1993) Racism: a concern for recreation resource managers, *Leisure Studies*, 9(4): 59–83.

Body-Gendrot, S. (2004) Race, a word too much? The French dilemma, in M. Bulmer and J. Solomos (eds), *Researching Race and Racism*. London: Routledge.

Body-Gendrot, S. and Duprez, D. (2002) Sercurity and prevention policies in France in the 1990s: French cities and security, in P. Hebberecht and D. Duprez (eds), *The Prevention of Security Policies in Europe*. Brussels: VUB Brussels University Press, pp. 90–127.

Bonilla-Silva, E. (1999) The new racism, in P. Wong (ed.), *Race, Ethnicity and Nationality in the United States*. Boulder, CO: Westview Press.

Bonnett, A. (1996) Constructions of 'race', place and discipline geographies of 'racial' identity and racism, *Ethnic and Racial Studies*, 19(4): 864–83.

Bonnett, A. (1998) How the British working class became white: the symbolic (re) formation of racialized capitalism, *Journal of Historical Sociology*, 11(3): 316–40.

Bourdieu, P. (1984) *Distinction: A Social Critique of the Judgement of Taste*. Cambridge, MA: Harvard University Press.

Bourdieu, P. (1990) *The Logic of Practice*. Cambridge. Polity Press.

Bourgois, P. (2003) *In Search of Respect: Selling Crack in El Barrio*, 2nd edn. Cambridge: Cambridge University Press.

Bowling, B. and Phillips J. (2002) *Racism, Crime and Justice*. Harlow: Longman.

Brah, A. (1996) *Cartographies of Diaspora: Contesting Identities*. London: Routledge.

Brah, A., Hickman, M. and Mac an Ghaill, M. (eds) (1999) *Thinking Identities: Ethnicity, Racism and Culture*. Basingstoke: Macmillan.

Brewer, J. (2000) *Ethnography*. Buckingham: Open University Press.

Bromseth, J. (2002) Public places – private activities? Methodological approaches and ethnical dilemmas in research on computer mediated communication contexts, in A. Morrison (ed.), *Researching ICTs in Contexts Intermedia Report 3/2002*. Oslo: University of Oslo and Unipub Forlag, pp. 67–89.

Brown, M. (2000) Religion and economic activity in the South Asian population, *Ethnic and Racial Studies*, 23(6): 1045–69.

Brubaker, R., Loveman, M. and Stamov, P. (2004) Ethnicity as cognition, *Theory and Society*, 33: 31–64.

Brush, P. (2001) Problematizing the race consciousness of women of color, *Signs*, 27(1): 171–98.

Bulmer, M. (1991) W. E. B. DuBois as a social investigator: the Philadelphia negro 1899, in M. Bulmer, K. Bales and K. K. Sklar (eds), *The Social Survey in Historical Perspective 1880–1940*. Cambridge: Cambridge University Press.

Bulmer, M. and Solomos, J. (1996) Introduction: race, ethnicity and curriculum, *Ethnic and Racial Studies*, 19(4): 777–88.

Bulmer, M. and Solomos, J. (1999) *Racism*. Oxford: Oxford University Press.

Bulmer, M. and Solomos, J. (eds) (2004) *Researching Race and Racism*. London: Routledge.

Burkett, I. (1997) Social relationships and emotions, *Sociology*, 31(1): 37–55.

Burrows, R. and Gane, N. (2006) Geodemographics software and class, *Sociology*, 40(5): 793–812.

Butler, J. (1994) Against proper objects, *Differences: A Journal of Feminist Cultural Studies*, 6(2 and 3): 1–26.

Byrman, A. (2008) *Social Research Methods*. Oxford: Oxford University Press.

Carter, B. (2000) *Realism and Racism: Concepts of Race in Sociological Research*. London: Routledge.

Cashmore, E. and Troyna, B. (1982) *Black Youth in Crisis*. London: Allen and Unwin.

Chamberlayne, P., Bornat, J. and Wengraf, T. (eds) (2000) *The Turn to Biographical Methods in Social Science: Comparative Issues and Examples*. London: Routledge.

Chaplin, E. (1994) *Sociology and Visual Representation*. London: Routledge.

Chow, R. (1996) Where have all the natives gone?, in P. Mongia (ed.), *Contemporary Postcolonial Theory: A Reader*. London: Arnold.

Clifford, J. (1988) *The Predicament of Culture*. Cambridge, MA: Harvard University Press.

Clifford, J. (1997) *Routes: Travel and Translation in the late 20th century*. Cambridge, MA: Harvard University Press.

Clifford, J. (2000) Taking identity politics seriously: 'the contradictory, stony ground. ... in P. Gilroy, L. Grossberg and A. McRobbie (eds), *Without Guarantees: In Honour of Stuart Hall*. London: Verso, pp. 94–112.

Clifford, J. and Marcus, G. (eds) (1986) *Writing Culture: The Poetics and Politics of Ethnography*. Berkeley: University of California Press.

Cohen, P. (1996) All white on the night? Narratives of nativism on the Isle of Dogs, in T. Butler and M. Rusti (eds), *Rising in the East*. London: Lawrence and Wishart, pp. 170–214.

Collins, P. and Butcher, B. (1983) Interviewer and clustering effects in an attitude survey, *Journal of the Market Research Society*, 25(January): 278–86.

Conley, J. M. and O'Barr, W. M. (1990) *Rules Versus Relationships: The Ethnography of Legal Discourse*. Chicago: University of Chicago Press.

Conti, G. (1997) Conducting research with communities of color, *Qualitative Research*, 12(4): 97–120.

Cotterill, P. (1992) Interviewing women: issues of friendship, vulnerability and power, *Women's Studies International Forum*, 15(5 and 6): 593–606.

Cox, T. and Nkomo, S. M. (1990) Invisible men and women: a status report on race as a variable in organizational behaviour research, *Journal of Organisational Behaviour*, 11(6): 419–31.

Crompton, R. (2006) *Employment and the Family: The Reconfiguration of Work and Family Life in Contemporary Societies*. Cambridge: Cambridge University Press.

Crompton, R. (2008) Response to Savage and Burrows, *Sociology*, forthcoming.

Crompton, R. and Lyonette, C. (2007) Reply to Hakim, *The British Journal of Sociology*, 58(1): 133–4.

Daniel, W. W. (1969) *Racial Discrimination in England: Based on the PEP Report*. Harmondsworth: Penguin.

Dardar, A. and Torres, R. D. (2004) *After Race: Racism after Multiculturalism*. New York: New York University Press.

De Andrade, M. A. (2000) Ascertainment issues in variance components models, *Genet Epidemiology*, 19: 333–44.

De Vaus, D. (2002) *Surveys in Social Research*. London: Routledge.

Deloria, V. (1991) Native knowledge, *American Journal of Sociology*, 45(4): 89–120.

Denzin, N. K. (1997) *Interpretative Ethnography: Ethnographic Practices for the 21st Century*. Thousand Oaks, CA: Sage.

Derrida, J. (1976) *On Grammatology*, trans. G. Chakravorty Spivak. Baltimore: John Hopkins University Press.

Derrida, J. (1981) *Positions*. Chicago: University of Chicago Press.

DeVault, M. (1995) Ethnicity and expertise: racial and ethnic knowledge in sociological research, *Gender and Society*, 9(5): 612–31.

Dillman, D. A. (1991) The design and administration of mail surveys, *Annual Review of Sociology*, 17: 225–49.

Dillman, N. A. (2000) *Mail and Internet Surveys: The Tailored Design Method*. New York: Wiley.

DuBois, W. E. B. (1995) *The Souls of Black Folk*. New York: Signet Books.

Dula, A. (1997) Bearing the brunt of new regulation, *Hasting Centre Report*, 27: 11–12.

Dunbar Jr, C., Rodriguez, D. and Parker, L. (2002) Race, subjectivity and the interview process, in J. Gubrium and J. Holstein (eds), *Handbook of Interview Research: Context and Method*. Thousand Oaks, CA: Sage, pp. 279–98.

Duneier, M. (1992) *Slim's Table: Race, Respectability and Masculinity*. Chicago: University of Chicago Press.

Duneier, M. (1999) *Sidewalk*. New York: Farrar Straus and Giroux.

Duneier, M. (2004) Three rules I go by in my ethnographic research on race and racism, in M. Bulmer and J. Solomos (eds), *Researching Race and Racism*. London: Routledge, pp. 92–103.

Dunn, A. and Feather, G. (1998) Race and surveys, *Qualitative Research*, 8(3): 120–38.

Dunn, K. M., Klocker, M. and Salaby, T. (2007) Contemporary racism and Islamaphobia in Australia: racialising religion, *Ethnicities*, 7(4): 564.

Dyer, R. (1997) *White*. London: Routledge.

Dyson, S. (2001) Midwives and screening for haemoglobin disorders, in L. Culley and S. Dyson (eds), *Ethnicity and Nursing Practice*. London: Palgrave, pp. 149–68.

Edwards, R. (1990) Connecting method and epistemology: a white woman interviewing black women, *Women Studies International Forum*, 13(5): 477–90.

Edwards, R. (1998) A critical examination of the use of interpreters in the qualitative research process, *Journal of Ethnic and Migration Studies*, 21(1): 197–208.

Essed, P. (1991) *Understanding Everyday racism: An Interdisciplinary Theory*. Newbury Park, CA: Sage.

Essed, P. (2002) Everyday racism: a new approach to the study of racism, in P. Essed and D. T. Goldberg (eds), *Race Critical Theories*. Oxford: Blackwell Publishers.

Essed, P. (2004) Naming the unnameable: sense and sensibilities in researching racism, in M. Bulmer and J. Solomos (eds), *Researching Race and Racism*. London: Routledge.

Ethnic and Racial Studies (2006) *Ethnic and Racial Studies*, Special Issue *Ethnography*, 29(3).

Fanon, F. ([1961] 1968) *The Wretched of the Earth*. New York: Grove Press, Inc.

Fanon, F. ([1952] 1970) *Black Skins White Masks*. London: Paladin.

Fanon, F. (1986) *Black Skin, White Mask*. London: Pluto Press.

Feagin, J. R. (2000) *Racist America*. New York: Routledge.

Foucault, M. (1979a) *Discipline and Punish: The Birth of the Prison*. Harmondsworth: Peregine Books.

Foucault, M. (1979b) *The History of Sexuality*. London: Allen Lane.

Fowler, F. J. (2002) *Survey Research Methods*, 3rd edn. London: Sage.

Frankel, M. S. & S. Siang Ethical and Legal Aspects of Human Subjects Research on the internet http://www.aaars.org/spp/dspp/sfrl/projects/intres/main.htm (1999).

Frankenberg, R. (1993) Growing up white: feminism, racism and the social geography of childhood, *Feminist Review*, 45: 51–84.

Frankenberg, R. (1994) *The Social Construction of Whiteness: White Women, Race Matters*. Minneapolis: University of Minnesota Press.

Frankenberg, R. (2004) One unsteady ground: crafting and engaging in the critical study of whiteness, in M. Bulmer and J. Solomos (eds), *Researching Race and Racism*. London: Routledge.

Frosh, S., Phoenix, A. and Pattman, R. (2002) *Young Masculinities*. London: Palgrave.

Fryer, S. (1984) *Staying Power: the history of Black People in Britain*. London: Pluto.

Gajjala, R. (2002) An interrupted psotcolonial/feminist cyberethnography: complicity and resistance in the 'Cyberfield', *Feminist Media Studies*, 2(2): 177–93.

Gallagher, C. (2000) White like me? Methods, meaning and manipulation in the field of white studies, in F.W. Twine and J. W. Warren (eds), *Racing Research, Researching Race*. New York: New York University Press, pp. 67–92.

Gamble, D. (1993) Race in health studies, *Health and Fitness*, 24(5): 212–38.

Gandhi, L. (1998) *Postcolonial Theory*. Edinburgh: Edinburgh University Press.

Gatens, M. and Lloyd, G. (1999) *Collective Imaginings: Spinoza, Past and Present*. London: Routledge.

Geertz, C. (2000) *Available Light*. Princeton, NJ: Princeton University Press.

Gergen, K. J. (1994) *Realities and Relationships*. Cambridge: Harvard University Press.

Giddens, A. (1991) *Modernity and Self-Identity: Self and Society in the Late Modern Age*. Cambridge: Polity.

Gill, R. (1998) Dialogues and differences: writing, reflexivity and the crisis of representation, in K. Henwood, C. Griffin and A. Phoenix (eds), *Standpoints and Differences: Essays in the Practice of Feminist Psychology*. London: Sage, pp. 18–44.

Gilroy, P. (1987) *There Ain't No Black in the Union Jack*. London: Hutchinson.

Gilroy, P. (1993) *The Black Atlantic*. Cambridge, MA: Harvard University Press.

Gilroy, P. (1998) Race ends here, *Ethnic and Racial Studies*, 21(5): 838–47.

Gilroy, P. (2000) *Nations, Cultures and the Allure of Race: Between Camps*. London: Allen Lane.

Gilroy, P. (2001) *Against Race: Imaging Political Culture Beyond the Colour Line*. Cambridge, MA: The Belknap Press of Harvard University Press.

Gold, S. (1986) Ethnic boundaries and ethnic entrepreneurship: a photo-elicitation study, *Visual Sociology*, 6(2): 9–22.

Goldberg, T. (1993) *Racist Culture*. Blackwell: Oxford.

Goldthorpe, J. H. (2000) *On Sociology*. Oxford: Oxford University Press.

Government Statistical Service (1996) *Report on Census Data*. New York: Wiley.

Gubrium, J. F. and Holstein, J. A. (eds) (2002) *Handbook of Interview Research*. Thousand Oaks, CA: Sage.

Gunaratnam, Y. (2003) *Researching 'Race' and Ethnicity: Methods, Knowledge and Power*. London: Sage.

Hall, S. (1990) Cultural identity in the diaspora, in J. Rutherford (ed.), *Identity: Community, Culture and Difference*. London: Lawrence and Wishart, pp. 222–37.

Hall, S. (1991) Old and new identities, old and new ethnicities, in A. D. King (ed.), *Culture, Globalisation and the World System*. Basingstoke: Macmillan, pp. 75–90.

Hall, S. (1992) The West and the rest: discourse and power, in S. Hall and B. Gielben (eds), *Formations of Modernity*. Cambridge: Polity Press and The Open University, pp. 276–320.

Hall, S. (1993) Culture, community, nation, *Cultural Studies*, 7(3): 349–63.

Hall, S. (1996) Introduction: who needs identity? in S. Hall and P. du Gay (eds), *Questions of Cultural Identity*. London: Sage, pp. 1–17.

Hall, S. (2000) Conclusion: the multi-cultural question, in B. Hesse (ed.), *Un/settled Multiculturalism: Diaspora, Entanglements, Transruptions*. London: Zed Books, pp. 209–41.

Halsey, A. H. (2004) *A History of British Sociology*. Oxford: Clarendon.

Haraway, D. (1988) Situated knowledges: the science question in feminism and the privilege of partial perspective, *Feminist Studies*, 14(3): 575–99.

Harding, S. (ed.) (1987) *Feminism and Methodology*. Bloomington: Indiana University Press.

Harper, D. (1984) Meaning and work: a study in photo elicitation, *International Journal of Visual Sociology*, 2(1): 20–43.

Harrison, F. (1997) Anthropology as an agent of transformation, in F. Harrison (ed.), *Decolonising Anthropology: Moving Further Toward an Anthropology for Liberation*. New York: American Anthropological Association, pp. 1–16.

Hemmings, C. (2002) *Bisexual Spaces: A Geography of Sexuality and Gender*. London: Routledge.

Hertz, R. (1997) A typology of approaches to child care, *Journal of Family Issues*, 60(4): 62–89.

Hesse, B. (2000) Introduction: un/settled multiculturalism, in B. Hesse (ed.), *Unsettled Multiculturalisms: Diasporas, Entanglements, Transruptions*. London: Zed Books, pp. 1–30.

Hickman, M. (1998) Reconstructing deconstructing 'race': British discourses about the Irish in Britain, *Ethnic and Racial Studies*, 21(1): 288–307.

Higginbotham, E. (1992) African-American women's history and the metalanguage of race, *Signs*, 17(21): 251–74.

Hill Collins, P. (1993) *Black Feminist Thought: Knowledge, Consciousness and the Politics of Empowerment*. London: Harper Collins.

Holdaway, S. and O'Neill, M. (2006) Ethnicity and culture: thinking about 'police ethnicity', *The British Journal of Sociology*, 57(3): 483–502.

Holliday, R. (2000) We've been framed: visualising methodology, *The Sociological Review*, 48(4): 503–22.

Hollway, W. and Jefferson, T. (2000) *Doing Qualitative Research Differently: Free Association, Narrative and the Interview Method*. London: Sage.

Holstein, J. and Gubrium, J. (1998) Active interviewing, in D. Silverman (ed.), *Qualitative Research: Theory, Method and Practice*. London: Sage, pp. 113–29.

Holstein, J. A. and Gubrium, J. F. ([1995] 2004) *The Active Interview*. Thousand Oaks, CA: Sage.

Home Office (2001) *Community Cohesion: A Report of the Independent Review Team Chaird by Ted Cantle*. London: HMSO.

hooks, b. (1992) *Black Looks*. New York: Routledge.

Howard, W. (2006) Race and racism: towards a global future, *Ethnic and Racial Studies*, 29(5): 986–1003(18).

Huber, J. (1995) Centennial essay: institutional perspectives on sociology, *American Journal of Sociology*, 101: 194–216.

Hudson, J. M. and Bruckman, A. (2002) The creation of an Internet-based SLA community, *Computer Assisted Language Learning*, 15(2): 109–34.

Huntingdon, S. (1996) *The Clash of Civilisation*. London: Routledge.

Hutchinson, M. (1996) *Ethnicity*. London: Routlege.

Islam, I. (2000) East Timor: development outlook, *Journal of the Asia-Pacific Economy*, 5(1 and 2): 2–8.

Jackson, J. L. Jr, (2001) *Harlemworld: Doing Race and Class in Contemporary Black America*. Chicago: University of Chicago Press.

Jaschok, M. and Jingjun, S. (2000) 'Outsider within': speaking to excursions across cultures, *Feminist Theory*, 1(1): 33–58.

Jenkins, R. (1997) *Rethinking Ethnicity: Arguments and Explorations*. London: Sage.

Johnson, P. (2004) Making social science useful, *British Journal of Sociology*, 55(1): 23–30.

Jones, T. (1993) *Britain's Ethnic Minorities*. London: Policy Studies Institute.

Jones, S. G. (ed.) (1997) *Virtual Culture: Identity and Communication in Cybersociety*. London: Sage.

Jones, S. G. (ed.) (1999) *Doing Internet Research: Critical Issues and Methods for Examining the Net*. Thousand Oaks, CA: Sage.

Kalra, V. (2000) *From Textile Mills to Taxi Ranks: Experiences of Migration, Labour and Social Change*. Ashgate: Aldershot.

Kandelwal, M. S. (2002) *Becoming American, Being Indian: An Immigrant Community in New York*. New York: Cornell University Press.

Kim, C. J. (1999) The racial triangulation of Asian Americans, *Politics and Society*, 27(1): 105–38.

Kincheloe, J. L and Steinberg, S. R. (eds) (1998) *Unauthorised Methods*. London: Routledge.

Knowles, C. (1999) Race, identities and lives, *Sociological Review*, 47(1): 110–35.

Knowles, C. (2003) *Race and Social Analysis*. London: Sage.

Knowles, C. (2005) Making whiteness: British lifestyle migrants in Hong Kong, in C. Alexander and C. Knowles (eds), *Making Race Matter: Bodies, Space and Identity*. Basingstoke: Palgrave Macmillan, pp. 90–110.

Knowles, C. (2006) Seeing race through the lens, *Ethnic and Racial Studies*, 29(3): 512–29.

Kvale, S. (1996) *InterViews*. London: Sage.

Labov, W. and Fanshel, D. (1977) *Therapeutic Discourse*. New York. Academic Press.

Ladner, J. ([1973] 1998) *The Death of White Sociology: Essays in Race and Culture*. Baltimore: Black Classic Press.

Lamont, M. (1992) *Money, Morals, and Manners: The Culture of the French and the American Upper-Middle Class*. Chicago, IL: University of Chicago.

Lamont, M. (2000) *The Dignity of Working Men: Morality and the Boundaries of Race, Class and Immigration*. Cambridge, MA, and New York: Harvard University Press and Russell Sage Foundation.

Lamont, M. (2002) *The Dignity of Working Men*. Cambridge, MA: Harvard University Press.

Lamont, M. (2004) A life of sad, but justified, choices: interviewing across (too) many divides, in M. Bulmer and J. Solomos (eds), *Researching Race and Racism*. London: Routledge, pp. 162–71.

Lather, P. (2001) Postbook: working the ruins of feminist ethnography, *Signs*, 27(1): 199–227.

Lather, P. (2001) Postmodernism, post-structuralism and post (critical) ethnography: of ruins, aporias and angels, in P. Atkinson, A. Coffey, S. Delamont, J. Lofland and L. Lofland (eds), *Handbook of Ethnography*. London: Sage, pp. 477–92.

Latour, B. (1983) Give me a laboratory and I will raise the world, in K. Korr-Cetina and M. Mulkay (eds), *Science Observed: Perspectives in the Social Study of Science*. London: Sage, pp. 141–70.

Latour, B. (1987) *Science in Action: How to Follow Scientists and Engineers Through Society*. Cambridge, MA: Harvard University Press.

Latour, B. (2005) *Reassembling the Social: An Introduction to Actor-Network Theory*. Oxford: Oxford University Press.

Lauder, H., Brown, P. and Halsey, A. (2004) Sociology and political arithmetic: some principles of a new policy science, *The British Journal of Sociology*, 55(1), 3–22.

Lawrence, E. (1982) In the abundance of water, the fool is thirsty: sociology and black pathology, *CCCS: The Empire Strikes Back*. London: Hutchinson, pp. 190–219.

Letherby, G. (2005) *Current Issues and Future Trends in Sociology: Extending the Debate in Sociological Research Online*, 10(1). Available at: http://www.socresonline.org.uk/10/1/letherby.html

Levine, P. (2000) Orientalist sociology and the creation of colonial sexualities, *Feminist Review*, 65: 5–21.

Lewis, G. (2000) *Race, Gender, Social Welfare: Encounters in a Postcolonial Society*. London: Routledge.

Lieberson, S. (1980) *A Piece of the Pie: Blacks and White Immigrants since 1880*. Berkeley: University of California Press.

Lieberson, S. and Waters, M. (1988) *From Many Strands: Ethnic and Racial Groups in Contemporary America*. New York: Russell Sage Foundation.

Liebow, E. (1967) *Tally's Corner: A Study of Negro Street Corner Men*. Boston: Little, Brown and Co.

Lindley, J. (2002) Race or religion? The impact of religion on the employment and earnings of Britain's ethnic communities, *Journal of Ethnic and Migration Studies*, 28(3): 427–42.

Loewen, J. W. (1971) *The Mississippi Chinese: Between Black and White*. Cambridge, MA: Harvard University Press.

Lorde, A. ([1979] 1981) The Master's tools will never dismantle the Master's house. Comments at 'The Personal and the Political' Panel, Second Sex Conference, in C. Moraga and G. Anzaldua, *This Bridge Called my Back*. New York: Kitchen Table Omen of Color Press, pp. 98–101.

Lorimer, D. (1978) *Colour, Class and the Victorians: English Attitudes to the Negro in the Mid-Nineteenth Century*. Leicester: Leicester University Press.

Loury, G. C. (2002) *The Anatomy of Racial Inequality*. Cambridge: Harvard University Press.

Loury, G. C., Modood, T. and Teles, S. M. (eds) (2005) *Ethnicity, Social Mobility and Public Policy: Comparing the U.S. and U.K.* Cambridge: Cambridge University Press.

Malik, K. (1996) *The Meaning of Race: Race, History and Culture in Western Society*. Basingstoke: Macmillan.

Malinowski, M. (1922) *Argonauts of the Western Pacific*. New York: E. P. Dutton.

Mani, L. (1990) Multiple mediations: feminist scholarship in the age of multinational reception, *Feminist Review*, 35(4): 25–38.

Mann, C. and Stewart, F. (2000) *Internet Communication and Qualitative Research: A Handbook for Researching Online*. London: Sage.

Marcus, G. (1986) Contemporary problems of ethnography in the modern world system, in G. Marcus and J. Clifford (eds), *Writing Culture: The Poetics and Politics of Ethnography*. Berkeley: University of California Press.

Marcus, G. (1998) *Ethnography Through Thick and Thin*. Princeton, NJ: Princeton University Press.

Marcus, G. and Clifford, J. (eds) (1986) *Writing Culture: The Poetics and Politics of Ethnography*. Berkeley: University of California Press.

Markman, A. (1998) *Life Online: Researching Real Experience in Virtual Space*. Walnut Creek, CA: AltaMira Press.

Marshall, H., Woollett, A. and Dosanjh, N. (1998) Researching marginalized standpoints: some tensions around plural standpoints and diverse 'experiences', in K. Henwood, C. Griffin and A. Phoenix (eds), *Standpoints and Differences: Essays in the Practice of Feminist Psychology*. London: Sage, pp. 115–34.

Martiniello, M. (2001) Is there a Belgian School of Ethnic and Migration Studies?, in P. Ratcliffe (ed.), *The Politics of Social Science Research*. Basingstoke: Palgrave.

Mason, D. (1994) On the dangers of disconnecting race and racism, *Sociology*, 28(4): 845–58.

Mason, D. (1996) Themes and Issues in the teaching of race and ethnicity, *Ethnic and Racial Studies*, 19(4): 789–806.

May, C. (2005) Methodological pluralism, British sociology and the evidence-based state: a reply to Payne et al., *Sociology*, 39(3): 519–28.

McAvoy, L., Winter, P. L., Outley, C. W., McDonald, D. and Chavez, D. J. (2000) Conducting research with communities of color, *Society and Natural Resources*, 13(5): 479–88.

McClintock, A. (1995) *Imperial Leather: Race, Gender and Sexuality in The Colonial Contest*. New York: Routledge.

McCracken, G. (1988) *The Long Interview*. London: Sage.

McDonald, R. (2001) *Designing Qualitative Research*. Boston, MA: Harvard University Press.

McDonald, D. and McAvoy, L. (1997) Native Americans and leisure: state of the research and future directions, *Journal of Leisure Research*, 29: 146–65.

Mercer, K. (1994) *Welcome to the Jungle*. London: Routledge.

Merry, M. (1990) Gender, race, and strategies of coping with occupational stress in policing, *Justice Quarterly*, 34(3): 78–102.

Merton, R. K. (1988) Some thoughts on the concept of sociological autobiography, in M. W. Riley (ed.), *Sociological Lives*. Newbury Park, CA: Sage, pp. 17–34.

Mihesuah, D. A. (ed.) (1993) *Natives and Academics Researching and Writing about American Indians*. Lincoln: University of Nebraska Press.

Miles, R. (1982) *Racism and Migrant Labour*. London: Routledge and Kegan Paul.

Miles, R. (1989) *Racism*. London: Routledge.

Miles, R. and Torres, R. (1996) Does 'race' matter? Transatlantic perspectives on racism after race relations, in V. Amita-Talai and C. Knowles (eds), *Resituating Identities: The Politics of Race, Ethnicity and Culture*. Peterborough: Broadview Press, pp. 24–46.

Miller, J. (2001) *One of the Guys: Girls, Gangs and Gender*. New York: Oxford University Press.

Mills, C. W. (1997) *The Racial Contract*. Ithaca, NY: Cornell University Press.

Modell, J. and Brodsky, C. (1994) Envisioning homestead: using photographs in interviewing, in E. M. McMahan and K. L. Rogers (eds), *Interactive Oral History Interviewing*. New York: Routledge, pp. 123–59.

Modood, T. (2005) *Multiculturalism*. London: Zed Books.

Modood, T., Berthoud, R., Lakey, J. et al. (1997) *Ethnic Minorities in Britain*. London: Policy Studies Institute.

Modood, T., Berthoud, R. and Nazroo, J. (2002) 'Race', racism and ethnicity: a response to Ken Smith, *Sociology*, 36(2): 419–27.

Mohanty, C. T. (1991) Under Western eyes: feminist scholarship and colonial discourses, in C. T. Mohanty, A. Russo and L. Torres (eds), *Third World Women and the Politics of Feminism*. Bloomington: Indiana University Press.

Mulholland, J. and Dyson, S. (2001) Sociological theories of 'race' and ethnicity, in L. Culley and S. Dyson (eds), *Ethnicity and Nursing Practice*. London: Palgrave, pp. 17–38.

Murji, K. and Solomos, J. (eds) (2005) *Racialization: Studies in Theory and Practice*. Oxford: Oxford University Press.

Naples, N. (1996) A feminist revisiting of the insider/outsider debate: the 'outsider phenomenon' in rural Iowa, *Qualitative Sociology*, 19(1): 83–106.

Nayak, A. (1997) Tales from the darkside: negotiating whiteness in school arenas, *International Studies in Sociology of Education*, 7(1): 57–79.

Nayak, A. (2003) *Race, Place and Globalisation: Youth Cultures in a Changing World*. Oxford: Berg.

Nayak, A. (2006) After race: ethnography, race and post-race theory, *Ethnic and Racial Studies*, 29(3): 411–30.

Nebeker, R. (1998) Critical race theory: a white graduate student's struggle with this growing area of scholarship, *Qualitative Studies in Education*, 11(1): 25–41.

Omi, M. and Winant, H. (1994) *Racial Formation in the United States*, 2nd edn. New York: London.

Ong, A. (1999) *Flexible Citizenship*. Durham, NC: Duke University Press.

Oppenheim, A. N. (1992) *Questionnaire Design, Interviewing and Attitude Measurement*. London: Pinter Publishing.

Papadopoulos, I. and Lees, S. (2002) Developing culturally competent researchers, *Journal of Advanced Nursing*, 37(3): 258–64.

Payne, G. (2007) Social division, social mobilities and social research: methodological issues after 40 years, *Sociology*, 41(5): 901–17.

Payne, G. and Grew, C. (2005) Unpacking 'class ambivalence': some conceptual and methodological issues in accessing class cultures, *Sociology*, 39(5): 893–910.

Payne, G., Williams, M. and Chamberlain, S. (2004) Methodological pluralism in British sociology, *Sociology*, 38(1): 153–63.

Phoenix, A. (1994) Practising feminist research: the intersections of gender and 'race', in M. Maynard and J. Purvis (eds), *Researching Women's Lives from a Feminist Perspective*. London: Taylor & Francis.

Phoenix, A. (2001) Practising feminist research: the intersection of gender and race in the research process, in K. K. Bhavnani (ed.), *Feminism and Race*. Oxford: Oxford University Press, pp. 203–19.

Pickstone, J. (2000) *Ways of Knowing*. Manchester: Manchester University Press.

Pickstone, J. V. (2002) Ways of knowing: a new history of science, technology, and medicine, *Science and Public Policy*, 45(2): 109–30.

Pink, S. (2001) *Doing Visual Ethnography: Images, Media and Representation in Research*. London: Sage.

Pittenger, R. H. and Danehy, J. (1960) *The First Five Minutes*. Ithaca, NY: Paul Martineau.

Platt, L. (2005) *Migration and Social Mobility*. Bristol: Policy Press/Joseph Rowntree Foundation.

Platt, L., Simpson, L. and Akinwale, B. (2005) Stability and change in ethnic groups in England and Wales, *Population Trends*, 121, Autumn.

Poland, B. (2002) Transcription quality, in J. Gubrium and J. Holstein (eds), *Handbook of Interview Research: Context and Method*. Thousand Oaks, CA: Sage, pp. 629–49.

Potter, J. W. (1996) *An Analysis of Thinking and Research About Qualitative Methods*. New York: Lawrence Erlbaum.

Potter, J. and Wetherell, M. (1987) *Discourse and Social Psychology*. London: Sage.

Prashad, V. (2000) *The Karma of Brown Folk*. Minneapolis: University of Minnesota Press.

Pratt, M. L. (1992) *Imperial Eyes: Studies in Travel Writing and Transculturation*. London: Routledge.

Prior, L. (2003) *Using Documents in Social Research*. London: Sage.

Prior, L. (2004) Doing things with documents, in D. Silverman (ed.), *Qualitative Research: Theory, Method and Practice*. London: Sage, pp. 76–93.

Prosser, J. (ed.) (1998) *Image Based Research: A Sourcebook for Qualitative Researchers*. London: Falmer Routledge.

Punch, K. F. (2003) *Survey Research: The Basics*. London: Sage.

Radhakrishan, R. (1996) *Diasporic Mediations Between Home and Location*. Minneapolis: University of Minnesota Press.

Ramji, H. (2007) Dynamics of religion and gender among young British Muslims, *Sociology*, 41(6): 1171–89.

Ramji, H. (2008) Exploring commonality and difference in in-depth interviewing: a case-study of researching British Asian women, *British Journal of Sociology*, 59(1): 99–116.

Ratcliffe, P. (ed.) (2001) *The Politics of Social Science Research*. Basingstoke: Palgrave.

Ratcliffe, P. (2004) *'Race', Ethnicity and Difference: Imaging the Inclusive Society*. Maidenhead: Open University Press.

Rath, J. (2001) Research on immigrant ethnic minorities in the Netherlands, in P. Ratcliffe (ed.), *The Politics of Social Science Research*. Basingstoke: Palgrave.

Rattansi, A. (1994) 'Western' racisms, ethnicities and identities in a 'postmodern' frame, in S. Westwood and A. Rattansi (eds), *Racism, Modernity and Identity on the Western Front*. Cambridge: Polity, pp. 1–23.

Rattansi, A. and Westwood, S. (eds) (1994) *Racism, Modernity and Identity: On the Western Front*. Cambridge: Polity Press.

Ray, L. and Smith, D. (2000) Hate crime, violence and cultures of racism, in P. Iganski (ed.), *The Hate Debate*. London: Profile Books.

Reed, K. (2000) Dealing with differences: researching health beliefs and behaviours of British Asian mothers, *Sociological Research Online*, 4(4). Available at: www.socresonline.org.uk/4/4/reed.html

Reinharz, S. (1997) 'Who am I?' The need for a variety of selves in the field, *Reflexivity and Voice*. Thousand Oaks, CA: Sage.

Rhodes, P. J. (1994) Race of interviewer effects in qualitative research: a brief comment, *Sociology*, 28(2): 547–58.

Richardson, R. (1999) *Islamaphobia*. London: Runnymede Trust.

Riessman, C. (1987) When gender is not enough: women interviewing women, *Gender and Society*, 1(2): 172–207.

Riessman, C. K. (1993) *Narrative Analysis*. Newbury Park, CA: Sage.

Robson, C. (2007) *How to do a Research Project: A Guide for Undergraduate Students*. Oxford: Blackwell Publishing.

Rodriguez, N. M. (1998) Emptying the content of whiteness: towards an understanding of the relation between whiteness and pedagogy, in J. L. Kincheloe, S. R. Steinberg, N. M. Rodriguez and R. E. Chennault (eds), *White Reign: Deploying Whiteness in America*. New York: St. Martin's Press, pp. 238–69.

Roediger, D. (1994) *Towards the Abolition of Whiteness*. London: Verso.

Rogilds, F. (2006) How Charlie Nielsen was born, *Ethnic and Racial Studies*, 29(3): 530–42.

Root, M. (1992) *Racially Mixed People in America*. Newbury Park, CA: Sage.

Rosaldo, R. (1989) *Culture and Truth*. London: Routledge.

Rose, G. (2001) *Visual Methodologies: An Introduction to the Interpretation of Visual Materials*. London: Sage.

Rosenthal, G. (1993) Reconstruction of life stories: principles of selection in generating stories for narrative biographical interviews, in R. Josselson and A. Leiblich (eds), *The Narrative Study of Lives*. London: Sage, pp. 59–91.

Ruby, J. (2000) *Picturing Culture: Explorations of Film and Anthropology*. Chicago: University of Chicago Press.

Ryan, L. and Golden, A. (2006) 'Tick the box please': a reflexive approach to doing quantitative social research, *Sociology*, 4(6): 1191–200.

Ryen, A. (2002) Cross-cultural interviewing, in J. Gubrium and J. Holstein (eds), *Handbook of Interview Research: Context and Method*. Thousand Oaks, CA: Sage, pp. 335–54.

Said, E. (1978) *Orientalism*. London: Penguin.

Sapsford, R. (1999) *Survey Research*. London: Sage.

Savage, M. and Burrows, R. (2007) The coming crisis of empirical sociology, *Sociology*, 41(5): 885–1001.

Scheff, T. (1997) *Emotions, The Social Bond, and Human Reality: Part/Whole Analysis*. Cambridge. Cambridge University Press.

Schutte, O. (2000) Cultural alterity: cross cultural communication and feminist theory in North-South contexts, in U. Narayan and S. Harding (eds), *Decentring the Center – Philosophy for a Multicultural, Postcolonial and Feminist World*. Bloomington: Indiana University Press, pp. 47–66.

Scott, J. (1990) *A Matter of Record*. Cambridge: Polity Press.

Sears, D., Sidanius, J. and Bobo, L. (eds) (2000) *Racialised Politics: The Debate about racism in America*. Chicago, IL: University of Chicago Press.

Shibutani, T. and Kwan, K. (1965) *Ethnic Stratification*. New York: Macmillan.

Shields, R. (1996) Meeting and mis-meeting? The dialogical challenge to Verstehen, *British Journal of Sociology*, 47(2): 275–94.

Shosteck, H. (1977) Respondent militancy as a control variable for interviewer effect, *Journal of Social Issues*, 33(4): 36–45.

Shukla, S. (2005) *India Abroad*. New York: Cornell University Press.

Silverman, D. (2001) *Interpreting Qualitative Data: Methods for Analysing Talk, Text and Interaction*, 2nd edn. London: Sage.

Silverman, D. (ed.) (2003) *Qualitative Research: Theory, Method and Practice*. London: Sage.

Silverman, D. (ed.) (2004) *Qualitative Research: Theory, Method and Practice*, 2nd edn. London: Sage.

Simpson, J. (1996) Easy talk, white talk, talk back: some reflections on the meanings of our words, *Journal of Contemporary Ethnography*, 25(3): 372–89.

Simpson, S. (1997) Demography and ethnicity: case-studies from Bradford, *Journal of Ethnic and Migration Studies*, 23(1): 89–107.

Sivanandan, A. (1982) *A Different Hunger*. London: Pluto.

Sivanandan, A. (2006) Race, terror and civil society, *Race and Class*, 46(3): 1–8.

Smaje, C. (1997) Not just a social construct: theorising race and ethnicity, *Sociology*, 31(2): 307–27.

Small, S. (1989) Racial differentiation in the slave era: a comparative analysis of people of mixed race in Jamaica and Georgia. Unpublished PhD dissertation, University of California at Berkeley.

Small, S. (1994) Racial group boundaries and identities: people of mixed race in slavery across the Americas, *Slavery and Abolition*, 15: 17–37.

Small, S. (2004) Researching 'mixed-race' experience under slavery: concepts, methods and data, in M. Bulmer and J. Solomos (eds) *Researching Race and Racism*. London: Routledge, pp. 78–91.

Smith, A. W. (1993) Survey research on African Americans: methodological innovations, in J. H. Stanfield and M. Dennis (eds), *Race and Ethnicity in Research Methods*. Newbury Park, CA: Sage, pp. 217–29.

Smith, L. T. (1998) *Decolonising Methodologies: Research and Indigenous Peoples*. London: Zed.

Smith, L. T. (1999) *Decolonising Methodologies: Research and Indigenous Peoples*. London: Zed Books.

Smith, K. (2002) Some critical observations on the use of the concept of 'ethnicity', in Modood et al., *Ethnic Minorities in Britain*, *Sociology*, 36(2): 399–419.

Smith, S. M. (2004) *Photography on the Colour Line: W.E.B. DuBois, Race and Visual Culture*. Durham: Duke University Press.

Solomos, J. (2003) *Race and Racism in Britain*, 3rd edn. Basingstoke: Macmillan.

Solomos, J. and Back, L. (1994) Conceptualising racisms: social theory, politics and research, *Sociology*, 28(1): 143–62.

Solomos, J. and Back, L. (1995) *Race, Politics and Social Change*. London: Routledge.

Solomos, J. and Back, L. (1996) *Racism and Society*. Basingstoke: Macmillan.

Song, M. (2001) Comparing minorities' ethnic options: do Asian Americans possess 'more' ethnic options than African Americans? *Ethnicities*, 1(1): 57–82.

Song, M. (2004) Racial hierarchies in the USA and Britain: investigating a politically sensitive issue, in M. Bulmer and J. Solomos (eds), *Researching Race and Racism*. London: Routledge, pp. 172–86.

Song, M. and Parker, D. (1995) Commonality, difference and the dynamics of disclosure in in-depth interviewing, *Sociology*, 29(2): 241–56.

Spickard, P. (1989) *Mixed Blood: Intermarriage and Ethnic Identity in Twentieth Century America*. Madison: University of Wisconsin Press.

Spivak, G. C. (1987) *In Other Worlds: Essays in Cultural Politics*. New York: Methuen.

Spivak, G. C. (1990) Questions of multiculturalism, in S. Harasayam (ed.), *The Post-Colonial Critic: Interviews, Strategies, Dialogues*. New York: Routledge, pp. 59–60.

Spivak, G. C. (1992) The politics of translation, in Barrett and A. Phillips (eds), *Destabilising Theory: Contemporary Feminist Debates*. Cambridge: Polity Press, pp. 177–200.

Spivak, G. C. (1999) *A Critique of Postcolonial Reason*. London: Routledge.

St Louis, B. (2002) Post-race/Post-politics? Activist-intellectualism and the reification of race, *Ethnic and Racial Studies*, 25(4): 652–7.

Stanfield, J. (1993) Methodological reflections: an introduction, in J. Stanfield and R. Dennis (eds), *Race and Ethnicity in Research Methods*. Newbury Park, CA: Sage, pp. 3–15.

Stanfield, J. H. and Dennis, R. M. (eds) (1993) *Race and Ethnicity in Research Methods*. London: Sage.

Sudman, S. and Bradburn, N. (1974) *Response Effects in Surveys*. Chicago: Aldine.

Sudman, S. and Bradburn, N. (1982) *Asking Questions: A Practical Guide to Questionnaire Design*. San Francisco: Jossey-Bass.

Taylor, J. H. (1976) *The Half-Way Generation: A Study of Asian Youths in Newcastle Upon Tyne*. Lincoln: Nelson.

Thrift, N. (2005) *Knowing Capitalism*. London: Sage.

Tourangeau, R. and Smith, T. W. (1998) Collecting sensitive information with different modes of data collection, in M. Couper, R. P. Baker, J. Bethlehem et al. (eds), *Computer Assisted Surveys for Information Collection*. New York: Wiley, pp. 89–123.

Tracy, P. and Fox, A. (1981) The validity of randomized response for sensitive measurements, *American Sociological Review*, 46: 187–200.

Trinitivo, L. and Torres, R. D. (2004) Mapping comparative studies of racialisation in the US, *Ethnicities Guest Editorial*, 4(3): 307–14.

Trondman, M. (2006) Disowning knowledge: to be or not to be 'the immigrant' in Sweden, *Ethnic and Racial Studies*, 29(3): 431–51.

Troyna, B. (1995) Beyond all reasonable doubt? Researching 'race' in educational settings, *Oxford Review of Education*, 21(4): 395–408.

Turner, B. (1994) *Orientalism, Postmodernism and Globalisation*. London: Routledge.

Turner, B. S. (1996) *The Body and Society*. London: Sage.

Twine, F. W. (1996) Brown Skinned white girls: class, culture and the construction of white identity in suburban communities, *Gender, Place and Culture*, 3(2): 205–44.

Twine, F. W. (1998) *Racism in a Racial Democracy: The Maintenance of White Supremacy in Brazil*. New Brunswick, NJ: Rutgers University Press.

Twine, F. W. (2000) Racial ideologies and racial methodologies, in F.W. Twine and J. Warren (eds), *Racing Research, Researching Race*. New York: New York University Press, pp. 1–34.

Twine, F. W. (2006) Visual ethnography and racial theory: family photographs as archives of interracial intimacies, *Ethnic and Racial Studies*, 29(3): 487–511.

Twine, F. W. and Warren, J. (eds) (2000) *Racing Research, Researching Race: Methodological Dilemmas in Critical Race Studies*. New York: New York University Press.

Van Dijk T. A. (1993) Analysing racism through discourse analysis, in J. H. Stanfield and R. M. Dennis (eds), *Race and Ethnicity in Research Methods*. London: Sage, pp. 92–134.

Vaughan, D. (2005) On the relevance of ethnography for the production of public sociology and policy, *The British Journal of Sociology*, 56(3): 411–16.

Vaz, K. M. (1997) *Oral Narrative Research With Black Women*. London: Sage.

Venkatesh, S. (2000) *American Project: The Rise and Fall of a Modern Ghetto*. Cambridge, MA: Harvard University Press.

Venkatesh, S. (2002) 'Doin' the hustle: constructing the ethnographer in the American ghetto, *Ethnography*, 3(1): 91–111.

Vertovec, S. (2006) The emergence of superdiversity in Britain, Working Paper No. 25, Centre on Migration, Policy and Society and University of Oxford.

Visweswaran, K. (1997) *Fictions of Feminist Ethnography*. Minneapolis: University of Minnesota Press.

Wacquant, L. (2002) Scrutinizing the street: poverty, morality and the pitfalls of urban ethnography, *American Journal of Sociology*, 107(6): 1468–532.

Wacquant, L. (2006) *Body and Soul: Notebooks of an Apprentice Boxer*. Oxford: Oxford University Press.

Wacquant, L. (2007) *Urban Outcasts: A Comparative Sociology of Advanced Marginality*. Cambridge: Polity.

Walkerdine, V., Lucey, H. and Melody, J. (2001) *Growing Up Girl*. London: Palgrave.

Ware, V. (1992) *Beyond the Pale: White Women, Racism and History*. London: Verso.

Ware, V. (1993) *Beyond the Pale: White Women, Racism and History*. London: Verso.

Ware, V. (2005) The power of recall: writing against racial identity, in K. Murji and J. Solomos (eds), *Racialisation: Studies in Theory and Practice*. Oxford: Oxford University Press.

Warner, S. (1965) Randomized response: a technique for eliminating evasive answer bias, *Journal of the American Statistical Association*, 60: 884–8.

Waters, M. (1999) *Black Identities: West Indian Immigrant Dreams and American Realities*. Cambridge, MA: Harvard University Press and Russell Sage Foundation.

Watson, J. (1977) *In between Two Cultures*. Oxford: Basil Blackwell.

Wax, M. L. (1991) The ethics of research in American Indian communities, *American Indian Q*, 15(4): 431–56.

Webber, R. and Butler, T. (2006) Classifying pupils where they live, Working Paper No. 9, Centre for Spatial Analysis, University College London.

Wengraf, T. (2001) *Qualitative Research Interviewing: Biographic Narrative and Semi-Structured Method*. London: Sage.

Werbner, P. (1997) 'Essentialising Essentialism, Essentialising Silence: Ambivalence and multiplicity in the constructions of racism and ethnicity', in P. Werbner and T. Modood (eds), *Debating Cultural Hybridity: Multi-cultural Identities and the Politics of Anti-Racism*. London: Zed Books, pp. 226–54.

Wetherell, M. (1998) Positioning and interpretative repertoires: conversation analysis and post-structuralism in dialogue, *Discourse and Society*, 9: 431–56.

Wetherell, M. and Edley, N. (1998) Gender practices: steps in the analysis of men and masculinities, in K. Henwood, C. Griffin and A. Phoenix (eds), *Standpoints and Differences: Essays in the Practice of Feminist Psychology*. London: Sage, pp. 156–73.

Wetherell, M. and Potter, J. (1992) *Mapping the Language of Racism: Discourse and the Legitimation of Exploitation*. London: Harvester Wheatsheaf.

Whyte, W. F. (1943) *Street Corner Society: The Social Structure of an Italian Slum*. Chicago: University of Chicago Press.

Wieviorka, M. (2004) Researching race and racism: French social sciences and international debates, in M. Bulmer and J. Solomos (eds), *Researching Race and Racism*. London: Routledge.

Willis, P. and Trondman, M. (2000) Manifesto for ethnography, *Ethnography*, 1(1): 5–16.

Willott, S. (1998) An outsider within: a feminist doing research with men, in K. Henwood, C. Griffin and A. Phoenix (eds), *Standpoints and Differences: Essays in the Practice of Feminist Psychology*. London: Sage, pp. 174–90.

Wilson, W. J. (1974) The new black sociology: reflections on the 'insiders' and the 'outsiders' controversy, in J. E. Blackwell and M. Janowitzn (eds), *Black Sociologists: Historical and Contemporary Perspectives*. Chicago: University of Chicago Press, pp. 167–90.

Winant, H. (1994) *Racial Conditions*. Minneapolis: University of Minnesota Press.

Winant, H. (2000) The theoretical status of the concept race, in L. Back and J. Solomos (eds), *Theories of Race and Racism*. London: Routledge.

Winant, H. (2006) Race and racism: towards a global future, *Ethnic and Racial Studies*, 29(3): 986–1003.

Winter, S. (1998) *Researching Native Indians*. Chicago: University of Chicago Press.

Wooffitt, R. (2005) *Conversation Analysis and Discourse Analysis: A Comparative and Critical Introduction*. London: Sage.

Wuthnow, J. (2002) Deleuze in the postcolonial: on nomads and indigenous politics, *Feminist Theory*, 3(2): 183–200.

Young, R. (1995) *Colonial Desire: Hybridity in Theory, Culture and Race*. London: Routledge.

Young, A. A. (2004) Experiences in ethnographic interviewing about race: the inside and outside of it, in M. Bulmer and J. Solomos (eds), *Researching Race and Racism*. London: Routledge, pp. 187–202.

Zivot, L. (1979) Native American research, *Journal of Leisure Research*, 2(3): 123–49.

Index